Social and Economic Development in the Contemporary Arab Gulf States

This dissertation – consisting of the present volume and nine previously published articles, book chapters and a research paper – has been accepted on the 7th of September 2018 by the Academic Council at the Faculty of Humanities, University of Southern Denmark, for defence for the higher doctoral degree in philosophy.

Simon Møberg Torp
    Dean

The defence will take place on the 5th of April 2019

Martin Hvidt

Social and Economic Development in the Contemporary Arab Gulf States

University Press of Southern Denmark 2019

The author and University Press of Southern Denmark 2019
Printed by Narayana Press
Typesetting and cover by Dorthe Møller, Unisats Aps
Cover Photo: Martin Hvidt: Emirates Towers and Sheikh Zayed Road, Dubai

ISBN 978-87-408-3213-6

Social and Economic Development in the Contemporary Arab Gulf States
is published with support from:
University of Southern Denmark

University Press of Southern Denmark
55 Campusvej
DK-5230 Odense M
www.universitypress.dk

Distribution in the United States and Canada:
International Specialized Book Services
5804 NE Hassalo Street
Portland, OR 97213-3644 USA
www.isbs.com

Distribution in the United Kingdom:
Gazelle
White Cross Mills
Hightown
Lancaster
LA1 4 XS
U.K.
www.gazellebookservices.co.uk

Contents

	Acknowledgements	7
1	Introduction	11
1.1.	List of publications included in the Dissertation	14
2	Situating the Dissertation within its intellectual framework	17
2.1	Middle East Studies/Gulf Studies	19
	2.1.1 The transformation from Oriental Studies to Middle East Studies	20
	2.1.2 Institutionalization of Middle East Studies	21
	2.1.3 Topics of research	23
	2.1.4 Gulf Studies	25
	2.1.4.1 Scarcity of data	25
	2.4.1.2 A Distinct Theory	29
	2.4.1.3 Distinct research topics	33
	2.1.5 Conflicts and controversies within the field	35
	2.1.6 Institutionalization of Gulf Studies	36
	2.1.7 Summary	39
2.2	Area Studies epistemology	40
	2.2.1 Summary	45
2.3	Development Economics	47
	2.3.1 Growth Models	54
	2.3.2 Summary	55
2.4	Chapter summary	56
3.	Development in the Gulf states – Presentation of the enclosed articles and outline of key findings	59

Publication 1
Hvidt, Martin. 2004. "Limited Success of the IMF and the World Bank in Middle Eastern Reforms." *Journal of Social Affairs*. 21 (81): p. 77-103.   61

Publication 2
Hvidt, Martin. 2007. "Public – private ties and their contribution to development. The case of Dubai." *Middle Eastern Studies*. 43 (4): p. 557-577.   62

Publication 3
Hvidt, Martin. 2009. "The Dubai Model: An Outline of Key Development Process Elements in Dubai." *International Journal of Middle East Studies.* 41 (3): p. 397-418.   66

Publication 4
Hvidt, Martin. 2011. "Economic and Institutional Reforms in the Arab Gulf Countries." *Middle East Journal.* 65 (1): p. 85-102.   68

Publication 5
Hvidt, Martin. 2012. "Planning for Development in the Arab Gulf States: A content Analysis of Current Development Plans." *Journal of Arabian Studies.* 2 (2): p. 189-207.   71

Publication 6
Hvidt, Martin. 2013. *Economic Diversification in the GCC Countries – Past Record and Future Trends.* LSE Research Paper series no. 27: Kuwait Programme on Development, Governance and Globalisation in the Gulf States. London: The London School of Economics and Political Science (LSE). 51 pp.   74

Publication 7
Hvidt, Martin. 2015. "The State and the Knowledge Economy in the Gulf: Structural and Motivational Challenges." *The Muslim World.* 105 (1): p. 24-45   77

Publication 8
Hvidt, Martin. 2018. "The United Arab Emirates: Modernity and Traditionalism in Petroleum Sector Management." *In Public Brainpower: Civil Society and Natural Resource Management*, edited by Indra Overland, p. 311-328. Cham: Palgrave Macmillan.   80

Publication 9
Hvidt, Martin. Forthcoming. "Highly-skilled Migrants and their Contribution to Development: Exploring the nexus between the *Kafala* system, highly skilled migrants and societal growth in United Arab Emirates." *Journal of Arabien Studies.*   83

4   **Conclusion**   87

     References   92

5.   **Summary in Danish/Dansk resumé**   105

Acknowledgements

This dissertation has been a decade and a half in the making. Over this time-span I have benefitted from stimulating discussions and intellectual insight from a large number of people, to whom I owe my sincere gratitude.

First of all, thanks to my colleagues at the Centre for Contemporary Middle East Studies at the University of Southern Denmark for formal and informal discussions over the years related to the Middle East and not least for a work environment conducive to research: Martin Beck, Annabelle Böttcher, Dietrich Jung, Line Mex-Jørgensen, Martin Ledstrup, Sarah Louise Madsen, Mehmet Ümit Necef, Helle Lykke Nielsen, M.H. Ilias, Sofie Pedersen, Gry Hvass Pedersen, Torben Rugberg Rasmussen, Peter Seeberg, Kirstine Sinclair, Ahmed Abou El Zalaf, and finally our indispensable secretaries Lone L. Petersen and Pia Hansen.

A heartfelt thanks also to my former colleagues at Zayed University, College of Sustainable Sciences and Humanities (CSSH), where I held a professorship from 2013 to 2016. In particular, I want to thank my colleagues at the Department of Humanities and Social Sciences (HSS) with whom I was so fortunate to share an enjoyable and highly informative daily lunch break, where past and current reforms within the university and in society at large was a recurrent topic of discussion: Idil Akinci, Carla Bethmann, Sara Chehab, Justin Gibbin, Sabrina Joseph, Susanne Kranz, Mohammad Masad, Mehrdad Mozayyan, Anke Reichenbach, Tilde Rosmer, Rafael Reyes-Ruiz, Rima Sabban, Marta Wieczorek, and James Williams.

A special thanks to Abdullah Abdulkhaleq, a distinguished professor of political science at United Arab Emirates University, Al Ain for challenging my understanding of UAE. In the 2000s during my first several periods of field work he positively answered my requests for interviews, which always resulted in long and intense discussions related to the structure and dynamics of the UAE society.

Thanks also to the *Gulf Research Center*, formerly based in Dubai, for hosting me during several month-long research trips to those UAE from 2006 to 2012. It has been invaluable for my research to have this 'home-away-from-home' which not only provided a fully equipped office space but above all a group of researchers and practitioners with long working experience in the region whom I could always ask for advice, among them Christian Koch, Eckart Woertz, Mustafa Alani, and N. Janardhan.

I also want to thank the *Center for International and Regional Studies* (CIRS), Georgetown University, Qatar for twice inviting me to participate in their working groups (2013-2014 and 2016-2017). I have treasured these working groups because our meetings provided an exceptionally qualified, intense and committed forum for discussions and learning on the selected topics. Thanks to Mehran Kamrava and Zahra Babar for organizing and hosting these fora.

Thanks also to the close to 200 professionals within all six Gulf countries who responded positively to my request for an interview. The significant lack of written sources of social science related issues pertaining to the Arab Gulf countries has made it imperative that researchers have access to persons who have first-hand knowledge of the issues under study. I thank these persons for setting time aside in their busy schedules to answer my many questions. This study would not have been possible without their willingness to participate.

Thanks also to the Emirati students who attended my classes at Zayed University and who, with their comments, questions, discussions in class and not least written assignments, provided me with a, for an outsider, rare insight into how the next generation of Emirati decision-makers conceive of the challenges and opportunities faced by their society.

Finally, a lot of thanks and gratitude goes to my family, first and foremost to my wife Dr. Charlotte N. Wien with whom I, among a host of mutual interests, share the passion for the Middle East. I am deeply indebted to her for juggling her professional life in such a manner that it allowed us to travel together on some of the month-long field trips, and especially to make it possible to relocate to Dubai for a three-year period. However, my gratitude to her extends even further, to her inherent curiosity and ability to question observations. While being in the Arab Gulf region, we as a family ventured off weekend after weekend exploring the cities and villages, their souqs, their infrastructure, and not least the modern developments, while questioning, discussing, and interpreting the society and changes we saw. These ongoing discussions have been fundamental in forming my understanding of the Arab Gulf countries.

I have been fortunate enough to receive two sizeable research grants from the Danish Social Science Research Council, which in combination with my tenured position at the Center for Contemporary Middle East Studies at the University of Southern Denmark have made it possible to carry out the research and not least to conduct extensive field work in the Arab Gulf region. The two funded projects are: *Dubai: A Middle Eastern Developmental State*, August 2006 – December 2007, and the project *Gulf rising: Developmental patterns in the resource rich economies of the Arab Gulf Region*, August 2010 – July 2014, which allowed me to conduct field work in each of the six Gulf states.

1 Introduction

This higher doctoral dissertation takes the form of an anthology and encompasses the present volume and nine single-authored publications - listed at the end of this introduction. The included articles, book chapters, and a research paper are a selection of the publications, which originate in research carried out over the last decade and a half, or more precisely since 2003, when I first started to pay academic attention to the unique and highly puzzling development in the Arab Gulf states that could be observed.

What first caught my attention back then was the frantic creation of signature buildings, artificial islands, themed shopping malls, and spectacular sporting events spearheaded by the tiny city state of Dubai. However, as I studied this development process more intensely, my focus turned to the discrepancy between the rapidity of establishing the overt features of development, exemplified by the buildings, and the comparatively slow pace of changing the social and economic institutions that govern everyday life for the citizens.

Aerial photographs of the capital city in UAE, Abu Dhabi taken in 1955 show a village with only two stone buildings, the fort and the residence of the ruler, whereas the rest of the tiny population were settled around the fort in the so-called *barasti* houses, huts built of date palm fronds. Needless to say, the city had no paved roads, hospitals, schools, besides the *madrassa*, or any kind of basic amenities.[1] As the oil industry established

---

[1] These photographs are exhibited at the Qasr Al Hosn visitor centre in Abu Dhabi. See also Al-Fahims ([1995] 2007) autobiographical book *From Rags to Riches*, which reads as a leading merchant's observation of the development of Abu Dhabi in the 1950s, 60s and 70s.

itself, the city developed, and the population increased rapidly. From an estimated size of 10 000 inhabitants in 1939, Abu Dhabi had grown to a population of 46 000 at the first census in 1968 (Heard-Bey 2001, 100; Zahlan 1978, 4). And the growth has continued, today more than 2.5 million live there. The noteworthy point is that the development from a tiny and impoverished sea shore village to an affluent and modern city with a Hong Kong-like skyline and all thinkable amenities has taken place in a period of just around 60 years, implying that the living generation of grandparents is likely to have grown up under the above described conditions prevailing in the 1950s.

One of the puzzling questions in the development of Arab Gulf countries is how progressive and development-inclined rulers attempt to develop their countries, given a population that, only two generations back, basically had received no formal schooling, countries that have hardly experienced industrialization, and where the state functions and bureaucracy have developed only recently and alongside increasing oil revenues.

This exceptionally fast developmental process is the focus of this dissertation. In a developmental perspective, the Gulf countries are to be considered 'outliers' compared to development in poorer countries in Asia, Africa and Latin America. The Gulf countries have been relieved of one constraining factor, lack of capital. However, as will be evident, to be 'capital rich' solve some problems associated with development, but certainly not all.

The overall aim of this dissertation is to contribute theoretically and empirically to advance science within the scholarly field of social science-based Gulf studies through analyses of the social and economic development in the Arab Gulf states. More specifically this dissertation analyses selected aspects of the developmental trajectory of the Arab Gulf states – that is, how the patterns of economic change and structural transformation are manifested in each country (Cammett et al. 2015, 9).

This dissertation is multi-disciplinary by nature and is at the overall level situated between the academic disciplines of history and social sciences.[2] While the discipline of history has a long tradition within Middle East studies and especially in Gulf studies where it has produced notable insight into the historical development of the region, social sciences dealing with contemporary political, economic and social developments has been, and arguably still is, in its infancy both theoretically and em-

---

2   See e.g. Cavazza (2017) for a discussion of the overlap and interaction of the two scholarly fields.

1 Introduction

pirically primarily due a significant scarcity of data and lack of access to key expert sources. Relying on significant field work, the incorporation of a new type of data source, and the application of a theory new to this research field, this dissertation, I believe, is instrumental in advancing the field of social science-based Gulf studies at least a tiny step.

This dissertation has been inspired by, and conceived within, two specific scholarly fields. One is Middle East studies/Gulf studies, and the other development economics. In addition, this dissertation relies on a specific epistemological approach, i.e. area studies. The application of the area studies approach represents a deliberate choice by the author, but is at the same time the mainstream approach within Middle East studies and particularly in Gulf studies. Thus, the intellectual framework on which this dissertation relies can be depicted as three overlapping circles, where the research, figuratively speaking, lies within the overlapping area of the three circles.

Figure 1. The Intellectual framework of the dissertation

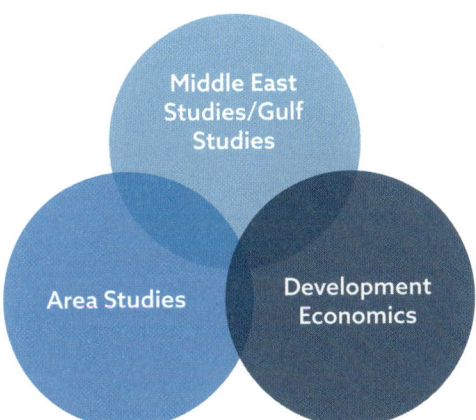

These traditions will be presented in more detail below but, for now, Middle East studies/Gulf studies define the overall research tradition, its paradigms, its theoretical approaches and its institutionalization; area studies represent a specific epistemological approach which is embedded in Gulf studies; and development economics, a discipline in social sciences, largely defines the topical enquiry, i.e. the focus on societal development and planning, the specific topics of the enquiry addressed in each publication and the theories and middle-range theories that were applied.

The present volume is organised in three parts. First an account of the intellectual framework of this study will be provided, consisting of reviews of the two scholarly fields and the area studies approach. The second part consists of a summary of the research findings encompassed in each of the included publications, which constitute this higher doctoral dissertation. The third part is a resume of the dissertation written in Danish.

1.1. List of publications included in the Dissertation

1. Hvidt, Martin. 2004. "Limited Success of the IMF and the World Bank in Middle Eastern Reforms." Journal of Social Affairs. 21 (81): p. 77-103.
2. Hvidt, Martin. 2007. "Public - private ties and their contribution to development. The case of Dubai." *Middle Eastern Studies.* 43 (4): p. 557-577.
3. Hvidt, Martin. 2009. "The Dubai Model: An Outline of Key Development-Process Elements in Dubai." *International Journal of Middle East Studies.* 41 (3): p. 397-418.
4. Hvidt, Martin. 2011. "Economic and Institutional Reforms in the Arab Gulf Countries." *Middle East Journal.* 65 (1): p. 85-102.
5. Hvidt, Martin. 2012. "Planning for Development in the Arab Gulf States: A content Analysis of Current Development Plans." *Journal of Arabian Studies.* 2 (2): p. 189-207.
6. Hvidt, Martin. 2013. *Economic Diversification in the GCC Countries - Past Record and Future Trends.* LSE Research Paper series no. 27: Kuwait Programme on Development, Governance and Globalisation in the Gulf States. London: The London School of Economics and Political Science (LSE). 51 pp.
7. Hvidt, Martin. 2015. "The State and the Knowledge Economy in the Gulf: Structural and Motivational Challenges." *The Muslim World.* 105 (1): p. 24-45.
8. Hvidt, Martin. 2018. "The United Arab Emirates: Modernity and Traditionalism in Petroleum Sector Management." In *Public Brainpower: Civil Society and Natural Resource Management*, edited by Indra Overland, 311-328. Cham: Palgrave Macmillan.

9. Hvidt, Martin. Forthcoming. "Highly-skilled Migrants and their Contribution to Development: Exploring the nexus between the *Kafala* system, highly skilled migrants and societal growth in United Arab Emirates." *Journal of Arabien Studies.*[3]

Throughout the dissertation, the enclosed publications will be referred to by the number they are given above, e.g., Publication 7.

Formally it should be mentioned that none of the publications included in this dissertation have previously been submitted for the purpose of obtaining an academic degree.

---

3 The article was submitted for publication on 28th of August 2018

2 Situating the Dissertation within its intellectual framework

As described above, the overall aim of this dissertation is to advance science within the scholarly field of social science-based Gulf studies. In this section, a historical, institutional and theoretical review of this scholarly field will be provided.

My research, or more precisely the research questions asked, the theories and methodologies applied and the approach(es) chosen have been conceived, formed and shaped by the interplay between not only the three elements in the intellectual framework provided above, but also in the dialectics between my research and the cumulative empirical and theoreticaly insight within the field of Gulf studies.

Thus, in addition to a review of the scholarly field of Gulf studies, this chapter includes an explication of the epistemological approach pursued, i.e. the one implied in area studies. This approach that dominates work within the scholarly field of Gulf studies emphasises multi-disciplinarity, value contextual (or particularistic) knowledge, and has less of a nomothetic aim than the pure disciplines. Furthermore, the research focus and methodology embedded in the scholarly discipline of development economics is reviewed to explicate how these have formed and shaped the research presented here.

In contrast to strictly discipline-oriented research, the theoretical universe implied in the academic field of Gulf studies is broader and does not lend itself to a review encompassing all applied theories and perspectives. Hence, for this review, I have chosen to single out the aspects of the scholarly field which I consider of most relevance for the studies conducted in this dissertation, implying that others are left untouched. In other words, there is no pretence to provide an exhaustive literature review of Gulf studies. The focus of the review will primarily be on the social science-based studies of the Gulf. Two additional reasons underpin this approach. First, and most importantly, each of the publications included in this dissertation encompasses a thorough review of the relevant literature, and second, extensive literature reviews exist for the scholarly field of Middle East studies, the specific theory of rentier states, and not least for development economics, rendering it superfluous to replicate such work.

The reason for this approach is that the aim of this dissertation is to advance science within a broad scholarly field namely that of Gulf studies, that is, not to a unique theory or set of theories.

Section 2.1 focuses on Middle East studies/Gulf studies, highlighting the young and immature stage that social science-based Gulf studies currently find themselves. The significant lack of data, one hegemonic theory and various distinct research topics distinguish the research field of Gulf studies from the broader field of Middle East studies.

Section 2.2 discusses area studies' epistemology. After the Second World War, area studies, especially in the American tradition, became the vehicle for transforming traditional Oriental studies into modern Middle East studies, which add social science-based research to the primarily humanistic field, and as a distinct difference from Oriental studies, aimed to deliver useful strategic advice. As mentioned above, area studies' epistemology emphasises multi-disciplinarity, value contextual (or particularistic) knowledge, and is less nomothetic than the pure disciplines. The author considers this approach both suitable and necessary for the study of the Arab Gulf societies and economies.

Section 2.3 focuses on the scholarly discipline of development economics. This sub-discipline of economics covers a broad range of topics believed to promote growth and development in non-industrialised countries; e.g., industrialization, urbanization, human capital, state and state planning, institutions, etc. Due to its broad reach, the academic field of development studies appears eclectic and lacking broader theoretical constructs. It is characterised by the existence of middle-range theories, each related to various topics and contexts. Development economics has formed the fundamental assumption of economic behavior, of state planning and how both growth and development are conceived for this study.

2.1 Middle East Studies/Gulf Studies

Only recently have Gulf studies emerged as a distinct scholarly field as manifested in the founding of its own scholarly organization, i.e. the Association for Gulf and Arabian Peninsula Studies (AGAPS) in 2011. Prior to that, research related to the Gulf countries was nested within the academic field of Middle East studies that emerged in America in the immediate aftermath of World War II and was a successor to the primarily European research field of Oriental studies.[4]

The academic study of the region that in the Anglo-American sphere is called Middle East and North Africa (MENA)[5] can be dated back to the beginning of the seventeenth century. During this century, it established itself as a distinct academic discipline within universities in central Europe, especially in France and Germany, under the name Orientalistik or Orientwissenschaft(en).[6] By the late 19th century, Germany had become a major center for such studies.

Lockman (2010, 103) defines orientalism and Oriental studies as "that branch of the humanities which studied something called the Orient from the beginning of recorded history until the present, including the predominantly Muslim lands of Asia usually conceived of as components of a distinctly Islamic civilization."

For the orientalist the object of study was the Islamic civilization, especially as it unfolded in its 'golden age' in the eighth, ninth, and tenth centuries (Lockman 2010, 68). The means to obtain knowledge of these societies was philology, the historical analysis and comparison of languages in written texts. Oriental studies have traditionally included the subdisciplines of Assyriology, Iranianology, Turkology, Osmanistik, Semitic languages and Arabic, Hebraic studies, and Islamic studies.

Oriental studies over time would become rather isolated and introvert-

---

[4] This historical overview is based on various sources, first and foremost Lockman's (2010) excellent book *Contending Visions of the Middle East: The history of Politics of Orientalism*. In addition Tessler, Nachtwey, and Bandas' (1999) introduction to their edited book *Area Studies and Social Sciences: Strategies for understanding Middle East Politics*; Khalidi's (2003) *The Middle East as an Area in an Era of Globalization*; Mitchell's (2004) *The Middle East in the Past and Future of Social Science* and Binders (1976) edited book *The Study of the Middle East – Research and Scholarship in the Humanities and the social Sciences*.

[5] For the origin and delimitations of the concept of Middle East and North Africa, see e.g., Anderson (2000, 11-5).

[6] The start of oriental studies as an academic discipline is normally accredited to the upstart of the École special des *langues orientales* in Paris in 1795, headed by Silvester de Sacy (Lockman 2010, 68).

ed and thus, changed little in form, research focus, and methodology. Even as late as the mid-twentieth century, it was believed that "A scholar with mastery of the main languages and classical texts of Islamic high civilization was still presumed to be able to pronounce on almost anything related to Islam, across vast stretches of time and space" (Lockman 2010, 103).

2.1.1 The transformation from Oriental Studies to Middle East Studies

Three important and interrelated changes took place in regard to the study of the Middle East in the immediate aftermath of World War II. First, the purpose or aim of the research area changed from its intrinsic value i.e. its humanistic, inward oriented and philology-centered focus on the past to contemporary policy-relevant social science-based studies. This shift manifested itself in the renaming of the research field from Oriental studies to Middle East studies. Second, the center of gravity for Oriental studies crossed the Atlantic, due to ample funding and vast institutional build up in America.[7] Third, the organizational and institutional setting of the research field changed, i.e. from discipline-oriented studies to the so-called area studies.[8]

In America, expertise of the world regions was in short supply right after the second World War. As pointed out by Khalidi (2003, 177), "there was no body of expertise in US on the history, culture, and economics of most other regions of the world" besides the few regions like Latin America, the Caribbean and the Philippines that previously had belonged to the US spheres of influence, and besides a small group of missionaries, businessmen, and diplomats. And especially concerning the Middle East, the situation looked bleak, as "no American academic employed full time at any university could claim to be an expert in the economics, sociology or politics of the modern Middle East" (Mitchell 2004, 82).

America's response to this lack of specialists was to transfer sizeable funds to the university system to educate a new breed of experts through language training, interdisciplinary research and teaching on the Middle East.[9] In sharp contrast to Oriental studies, Middle East studies

---

7 It is likely that the situation in post war Germany and the slow demise of colonial Britain, should be added to the list of reasons for this
8 Area studies will be discussed in section 2.2 below.
9 Modern Middle East studies is normally thought to commence in 1947 where Phillip Hitti created a program under Princeton's Department of Oriental languages and Literature called Near Eastern Studies which came to serve as a model for similar centres at other universities (Lockman 2010, 127).

were 'born', with the task of producing useable knowledge that could assist America in undertaking its role as World leader on the international scene, and not least, by controlling rivals in the Cold War.

The applied focus of Middle East studies, as it developed in America, incorporated, as mentioned above, the social science disciplines, e.g., politics, sociology, anthropology, and economics. Middle East studies not only benefitted from the theoretical insight and methodologies embodied in these, but became, as a research field, susceptible to the changes in theoretical considerations, focus and paradigms, etc., which occurred within the social sciences in general. Hence, Middle East studies were influenced by the major shifts in social science theory, which happened after WWII: modernization theory, radical or *dependencia* theory in the 1970s and early 1980s and the neo-classical counterrevolution commencing in the mid-1980s.[10]

Despite the rapid growth of this new discipline – especially in America after World War II, it only slowly displaced Orientalists and Oriental studies. While the research field moved toward a social science orientation and increased policy-relevance, a significant cohort of researchers especially in Europe but also in America who had been educated and trained in the Orientalist tradition, continued to practice as they had been educated to do.[11] However, with the publication of the book *Orientalism* in 1978 Edward Said was instrumental in moving the research field further away from its orientalistic roots, which had come under increasing criticism for its simplistic assumptions and Western-centric world views. Despite the heated debate of Said's book, the research field acknowledged this achievement in 2002 by awarding Edward Said the World Congress for Middle East Studies (WOCMES) Award for Outstanding Contributions to Middle Eastern studies. Despite this shift, Oriental studies continued to exist especially in Europe, however in a somewhat changed form now under the name of Islamic studies.

2.1.2 Institutionalization of Middle East Studies

Middle East studies institutionalised itself in various ways. In America, the field got its own organization in 1966, i.e. the Middle East Studies

---

10　These theoretical approaches will be presented in greater detail in section 2.3 below.
11　See Lockman (2010, 149ff) for the situation in America. In Europe a strong tradition for oriental studies continue to exist along with the field of Middle East Studies (Valbjørn 2009, 29). An overview of Oriental studies in Denmark is depicted in Valbjørn and Andersen (2005) and in the various contributions in Rump (2006).

Association (MESA), which currently holds a membership of around 2600 persons.[12] The association serves as an umbrella organization for thirty-nine affiliated organizations including the Association for Gulf and Arabian Peninsula Studies (AGAPS). The association organises a large annual (2000+ participants) conference in America and also publishes the *International Journal of Middle East Studies*.[13]

In Europe, the European Association for Middle Eastern Studies (EU-RAMES) was founded in 1990 and serves as an umbrella organization for research institutions and national research associations in Europe, e.g., British Society for Middle East Studies (BRISMES), the Association Française pour l'étude du Monde Arabe et Musulman (AFEMAM) or the Deutsche Arbeitsgemeinschaft Vorderer Orient für Gegenwartsbezogene Forschung und Dokumentation (DAVO), and the regional society, the Nordic Society for Middle Eastern Studies.[14] The EURAMES Info Services, which maintains a mailing list informing the scholarly community on upcoming conferences, jobs and other activities for the Middle East holds a mailing list of more than 6000 recipients.[15]

Furthermore, the research field has institutionalised itself through the World Congress for Middle Eastern studies (WOCMES), which held its first conference in Mainz in September 2002. Since then, the conferences have been held in Amman (2006), Barcelona (2010), Ankara (2014), and in Sevilla (2018). Before WOCMES commenced, the annual MESA conference was the *de facto* World Wide meeting place for scholars of the Middle East.

Despite the relative widening of the international reach of the Middle East studies through the WOCMES conferences and the existence of an International Association of Middle Eastern Studies, Middle East studies remain a very American/European discipline. While research units exist in Australia, China, India, Japan, and also in Latin America, the institutions and the bulk of the scholars and not least, the bulk of the published research comes out of America and Europe.[16]

---

12 More precisely 2634 members of which 417 are from outside America. Data reported at the MESA Members Meeting, held 20 November 2017, Marriott Wardman Park Hotel, Washington D.C.
13 See Mesa website: http://mesana.org/about/index.html, accessed 20 March 2017
14 For a full list of member societies see http://org.uib.no/smi/eurames/euraddr.html
15 See e.g. Eurames Info 04/2016
16 Discussion with Günter Meyer, who serves as President of EURAMES and of the International Association of Middle Eastern studies (IAMES) and is chairing the International Advisory Council of WOCMES, Washington D.C., 18 November 2017.

2.1.3 Topics of research

What topics do the Middle East researchers work on? The answer is, basically everything. Below is the list of the main themes that WOCMES has used as a template for the call for papers for the first four conferences. It is evident from that list that the focus of Middle East studies is on societies and cultures, and that engineering, natural sciences, and medicine are not part of the research field. The core disciplines are humanities and social sciences, which include the humanistic disciplines of archeology, history, philology, cultural and gender studies, Islamic studies, and the social science disciplines of anthropology, ethnography, politics (international relations), sociology, economics, and law.

The poster (see below) for the WOCMES 2014 event provides an indication of the research field of Middle East studies. The list depicts a research field that is all encompassing and thus, does not exclude any topics within humanities and social sciences. Furthermore, it provides an indication that the humanistic tradition of Islamic studies continues to figure prominent in the Middle East studies. A similar conclusion can be drawn from a review of the 51 pages long programme for the 2017 MESA Annual conference (MESA 2017).

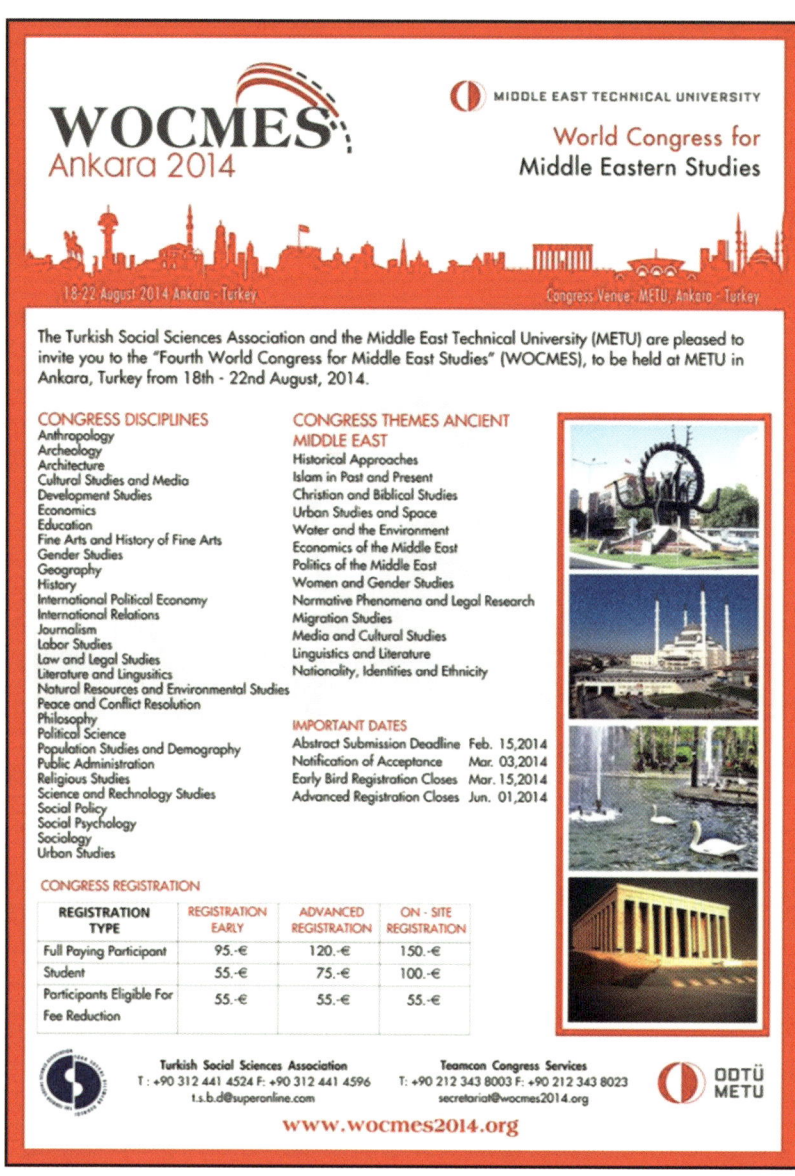

Figure 2. List of main themes for the WOCMES conferences

Erratum: In the second column, the heading is wrong. Should read only Conference themes. Ancient Middle East is an item belonging to the list below.

2 Situating the Dissertation within its intellectual framework

2.1.4 Gulf Studies

As mentioned, it is only recently (i.e. 2011) that Gulf studies branched off as a distinct sub-field within the broader scholarly field of Middle East studies, and consequently, scholars who have conducted research on the Gulf or are currently doing so, share the intellectual history and dominant research agendas pursued within Middle East studies.

While archeological, historical, and ethnographic studies of the region and its population were published throughout the 19th and 20th centuries, it is mainly within the last two decades that social science-based studies, especially those addressing domestic economic, social, and political issues within the countries of the region, have attained volume related to both publication output and the number of scholars involved in such studies.[17]

There are great similarities in, and overlaps between, the two scholarly fields of Middle East studies and Gulf studies, not least that History as a discipline is prominent in both of them. However, I will argue that social science-based Gulf studies, in the form it has been and is emerging at present, has three features that combined make it distinct from the broader discipline of Middle East studies, i.e. 1) the significant scarcity of data, 2) its distinct theoretical basis, and 3) its distinct set of research topics.

2.1.4.1 Scarcity of data

So far, Gulf studies are characterised by a significant scarcity of social science-oriented data.[18] While this is not unique to Gulf studies per se but more generally a challenge to research in most developing countries, it is arguably more significant in this region than in other places. Basic data, for example in relation to population size, nationality of labour force, national budgets, key economic data, income data, etc. are not readily available.[19] Even more scant and unsystematically collected are data at a less aggregated level, for example relating to income levels, education, or health systems, patterns of ownership of economic assets, transfer of

---

17 Examples of social science base studies on the Gulf region carried out prior to the 1990s: Beblawi and Luciani (1987); Crystal (1990); Gause (1990); Hudson (1977); Issawi (1970, 1982); Niblock (1980); Mallakh (1966); Zahlan (1978); Wilson (1987).
18 See e.g. Issawi (2004, 179ff) for a discussion of data issues pertaining to the Gulf States.
19 As an illustration, note that the CIA World Fact Book lists the population of the UAE at around 6 million (mid-2017) while the UN estimates the country's total population to be 9.4 million (also mid-2017). See World Fact Book, https://www.cia.gov/library/publications/the-world-factbook/geos/ae.html. The official statistical office in the UAE, the Federal Competitiveness and Statistics Authority, no longer provides their own numbers, but refers to the UNDP website for population statistics of the country. See http://fcsa.gov.ae/en-us/statistics/population-data-estimates. For a detailed discussion of data and data quality related to migrants, see Baldwin-Edwards (2011, 2ff).

social benefits, etc. With the unavailability of basic statistical data, the ability to use most types of statistical information and tools for research purposes are significantly limited. One consequence of this is that social science studies with a contemporary focus, including the studies in this dissertation, generally rely on qualitative methods, mostly interviews, as the primary tool for data collection.

As mentioned, while scarcity of data is certainly also a fact in other countries in the Middle East and for development studies more generally, I would argue that the issue is particularly manifest in the Gulf region due to four factors: the type of governance; the lack of capacity to collect data stemming from the fact that a system of taxation has not been established; the lack of outside involvement in the economy, i.e. through lending and membership of international organizations and international treaties; and finally, the predominance of an oral culture. In discussing these factors, one should bear in mind the very short time that has elapsed since the Gulf States engaged in their developmental drive.

According to the first factor, - the type of governance - at present, none of the Gulf countries are, nor strive to be, a 'democracy' in the sense of a liberal, Western multi-party system. The type of governance varies, but generally it relies on a traditional tribal governance system characterised by centralised decision-making, personalised rule, and consensus among the group of decision-makers, counterbalanced with the practice of consultation with the elites and tribal heads within society (Herb 1999, 31ff; Khalifa 1979; Gause 2010, Ch. 2; Van Der Meulen 1997, Ch. 2; Owen 2004, 39ff; Fox, Mourtada-Sabbah, and al-Mutawa 2006a). Phrased in social science terms, the type of governance is autocratic and neo-patrimonial and hence, does not encourage transparency in decision-making or public debate (e.g., in news media), let alone critique of decisions made (Publication 8). As a result, basic statistical data, if collected, are not published or made available to the public in other ways. As pointed out in Publication 5, decision-making on broader development issues does not generally leave a noteworthy 'paper trail' such as in the form of White Papers, newspaper columns, or minutes of parliamentary debates, which can inform a debate within society after decisions have been made. In addition, due to the nature of the governance form, generally there is an absence of organised interest groups, such as trade unions or political parties (however in Kuwait and Bahrain this is somewhat different) (Publication 8).

Furthermore, the access to the sources is related to the type of governance. In all of the Gulf States, a researcher formally needs a research permit issued by the respective government. Personally, I have not experienced problems in obtaining such permits in any of the Gulf countries, aside from Oman.[20] A greater obstacle to the researcher lies in the willingness of people to participate in interviews, possibly because social science research holds the potential to either raise critique directly or because the data and findings can be used by others to raise critique toward rulers and governments. The more sensitive the political situation is, the less likely it is that people wish to be interviewed, especially in relation to topics and issues that they might consider politically sensitive. This is true for both nationals and expats, and leads to people declining requests for interviews, or to interviewees declining to have the interview recorded, or to the interviewee asking to remain anonymous.[21] As an example, I have experienced marked shifts in the possibility of interviewing people in the Gulf region from before until after the financial crisis that commenced in 2008, from before until after February 2011 when the Arab spring took off, and lastly in 2015, when the UAE entered the war in Yemen alongside Saudi Arabia. Furthermore, discussions at the AGAPS 2017 Business Meeting expressed a concern for the deteriorating possibilities for doing field work in the region, following the new level of sensitivities resulting from the 'Qatar crisis.'[22]

The second reason for the scarcity of data relates to state capacity. Due to the vast incomes from the export of hydrocarbons, none of the Gulf countries, so far, has been forced to collect taxes to fund their public budgets.[23] Taxation necessitates systematic collection of information on the constituents of society, i.e. citizens, businesses, and financial institutions, in order for the state to make everyone contribute to the public purse (Hertog 2010, 265; Hvidt 1996, 86ff). As there has been no pressure to build such 'extractive' mechanisms, all governments in the region possess a weak capacity to collect and process data.

---

20 Oman is the least studied of the Gulf states (Tétreault, Kapiszewski, and Okruhlik 2011, 3). Anecdotally, it is known that Oman has denied nearly all research permits for the last 30 years, which has left Oman as one of the least studied countries in the world.
21 See, for example, Karen Young who in the acknowledgements of her 2014 book wrote: "I do not name these sources in the book because to do so would risk too much for me and for them. This is the weakest aspect of the book and a very telling one, as the borders of finance, state security and information are permeable and toxic in the UAE, as well as in the realm of corporate finance globally" (Young 2014)
22 AGSPS General Business Meeting, Marriott Wardman Park Hotel, Washington D.C., 18 November 2017.
23 Fees for various services, for example registration of a vehicle, hiring a domestic helper, etc. have so far been collected, but no systematic taxation has been undertaken.

The third reason for the lack of data is that the oil rich Gulf countries live in relative isolationism. As documented in Publication 1, the Gulf countries generally do not take loans from international financial institutions, i.e. the World Bank or the IMF, and thus are not obliged to align their accounting practices and procedures to world standards and, of equal importance, to be transparent, i.e. to disclose key financial and social figures. Furthermore, as documented by Hendrix and Noland (2014, Ch. 4) an inverse relationship exists between incomes from natural resources and the level of participation in international organizations and treaties. They argue that the resource rich states are characterised by 'unbalanced globalization,' meaning that these states display a high degree of economic integration in the world economy through trade but with comparatively poor integration in international organizations in which global governance takes place. With fewer memberships in such standards-based and political organizations and with participation in fewer international agreements and treaties, the necessity to collect and disseminate reliable data about their societies is reduced.

The final reason why acquiring good-quality data for research is especially difficult in the Arab Gulf states is that an oral culture has prevailed until very recently. Up until the mid-1960s, much governance would take place 'in front of the Fort.' That is, as daily or frequent public audiences where the ruler would make himself accessible to the people and exercise his rule through judgment of the cases brought before him. Furthermore, in an interview with the historian and lifetime researcher on the UAE, Dr. Frauke Heard-Bey in 2010, she highlighted the lack of tradition among Sheiks or other office holders in the UAE and in the other Gulf countries to either make or keep records. In fact, the tradition was for new sheikhs or officeholders to burn the archives of their predecessor when assuming their position. Furthermore, she pointed out that written archives would deteriorate fast due to the humid and warm climate.[24] Both factors leave the researchers with extraordinarily few written records to base their studies on.

An exception to this is the records kept by the British colonial administration. The British, who *de facto* ruled the Gulf from 1820 to 1971, kept extensive archives on the political, economic, and trade-related features of the societies they commanded. The foremost example of the diligence with which the British collected information is J. C. Lorimer's *Gazetteer of the Persian Gulf, Oman and Central Arabia*, a 6,000-page study published

---

24   Interview with Frauke Heard-Bey, Abu Dhabi, 24 November 2010.

in 1915 which summarises the history, the economy, the trade, and the security issues of the entire region from the arrival of the Portuguese to the Gulf in 1498 to 1910 (Lorimer [1915] 2003). The administrative procedures and the diligence of the British officers leave the scholarly world in a situation where the primary sources to the formative period of the current Gulf States (to a lesser degree Saudi Arabia and Kuwait) are written by the British and rest in various British archives, for example the British Library in London and the Institute for Arab and Islamic Studies, University of Exeter, which houses The Arab World Documentation Unit.[25]

The scarcity of contemporary social and economic data pertains to all six Gulf states and, as argued above, originate in both political and practical reasons. As mentioned, this scarcity of data has forced the researchers with a contemporary social science focus to rely methodologically on interviews, data collected from news media sources, and the limited academic writings available.

All this said, the data quality and availability has improved over the last decade, but remains a key challenge for social science researchers. Examples of improvements in macro level data are the data made available by the Gulf Labour Markets and Migration project (GLMM), in the various Arab knowledge Reports published by UNDP, the annual Global Competitiveness Report published by World Economic Forum, and the World Development Indicators published by the World Bank. However, no data are better than their sources!

In a recent book, Kropf (2016) set forth to conduct an econometric study of the growth and diversification in the Arab Gulf states. This study "should be perceived as a first step towards a more systematic and methodologically-focused approach towards the political economy of the Middle East, which is still mostly a domain of qualitative research" (Kropf 2016, 11). In the concluding chapter she discusses data insufficiency and concludes that the methodology of the study is indeed useful "if data one day becomes adequate" (Kropf 2016, 201).

2.4.1.2 A Distinct Theory

A distinguishing feature of social science-based Gulf studies is the reliance on one overriding theory, i.e. rentier state theory (RST) to explain economic and political behaviour of the states and their citizens. The theory was first conceived by Mahdavy in 1970 dealing with Iran, but was

---

25 See also the literature review on the economic and political development in the UAE in Ulrichsen (2017, Ch. 1).

subsequently expanded and popularised by Luciani and Beblawi, respectively, in two chapters in their edited book *The Rentier State* published in 1987 (Mahdavy 1970; Beblawi 1987; Luciani 1987).[26] However, even though we refer to RST as a theory, RST as pointed out by Hertog (2010, 264-5) does not form a coherent theory but exists as "a cluster of hypotheses on the impact of oil on politics and development in developing countries, postulating a variety of mostly negative effects." [27]

An obvious reason why the theory has become hegemonic in Gulf studies[28] is that whereas elements of rentierism exists in most countries, the Arab Gulf states appear as the archetypical rentier states (Herb 1999, 256) in that more than 80-90% of the states' income is derived from oil and gas (Publication 6 p. 13). Or as phrased by Beblawi (1987, 53), the Arab Gulf states represent, "the example *par excellence* of rentier states." In addition, the tribal/kinship nature of governance that dominates in the region underpin the effects of rentierism.

Fundamentally, RST analyses the effect of the influx of vast 'unearned' income or 'rents' on an economy. The theory holds three basic claims: First, that economic rent, e.g., originating from extraction – not production – of natural resources like oil or gas has a disruptive effect on the economy, through various mechanisms, e.g., Dutch disease or a 'crowding out' process. Both factors contribute to a decrease in productive efficiency in society. In the Gulf context 'crowding out' holds especially harmful prospects because it does not only imply that locally produced goods are challenged by imported products but more fundamentally, that the Gulf states, which at the advent of oil were underdeveloped and impoverished trading, fishing, and farming communities, along their developmental process largely have neglected to establish or facilitate productive sectors and activities.

For Luciani (1987, 74-5), the key feature of the allocation state (rentier states) is that such states do not need to levy taxes within society to finance state functions, implying that such states have little incentive to facilitate the growth of productive economic activities. In other words, such states are independent of the strength of their domestic economy. Furthermore, this leads to the argument that the only preoccupation of the state is to maximise the income from its sale of hydrocarbons, which has little to do with the domestic economy, and to distribute money with-

---

26 The book chapters by Beblawi and Luciani were reprinted in 1990 in their edited book: *The Arab State* (London: Routledge). The book chapters from 1987 and 1990 are identical. Throughout my studies, I have referred to the 1990 version of the chapters.
27 For a similar argument see also Kropf (2016, 99).
28 See e.g. Herb (1999, 256).

in society. Hence, in RST agency of the state is very limited. The broader arguments concerning the negative effects of rents are summarised in the so-called Resource Curse literature (see e.g. Auty 2001; Hendrix and Noland 2014; Herb 2017; Gylfason 2001; Luciani 2012). In recognizing the disruptive effects on the economies, Kuburi (1999, 311) in an older publication goes as far as to label oil 'the Arab Disease.'

The second claim by RST is that a rentier economy fosters a special mindset among both citizens and elites termed 'rentier mentality' (Beblawi 1987, 52ff). Plentiful incomes from the sales of hydrocarbons allow the individual ruler or government to generously distribute money within society leading to a break in the causation between 'work' and 'reward.' If reward, e.g., in the form of salary or status, is disconnected from the type or quality of the work being done or the effort that is put into it, and instead is related to luck (e.g., cash hand-outs or debt forgiveness, free housing), then society provides the individual with few incentives to pursue productive efficiency, i.e. to work hard, to engage in long and challenging educational activities, or apply a long-term perspective in climbing a career ladder. Hence, RST claims that the rational conduct in such societies is to optimise the access to the rent circuit rather than seeking productive efficiency (Chatelus 1990, 102). To illustrate, Gardner (2011) provides a detailed account of this optimization process in his analysis of the logic behind the stereotype of the 'Lazy Arab.' As Beck (2007, 46) points out, this leads to a situation, where massive oil rents can translate into a stabilization of economic inefficiency.

The third claim of RST relates to political representation and the resilience and longevity of the Gulf monarchies. The theory holds that societies characterised by a sizeable influx of rents tend to develop and sustain a type of governance that is authoritarian/autocratic. Without taxation, governments do not need to bargain with the population, and thus, rentier states are supposed to be relatively autonomous from societal demands, implying that they can spend the oil income at will and without being accountable to society (Hertog 2010, 265). Mayhew's 18th century slogan 'no taxation without representation' is adopted within RST to explain the persistence of autocratic governance in rent-based economies.

However, in a Gulf Arab context which is predominantly kindship/tribal based and patrimonial in nature the autonomous element of the state is modified by the existence of a 'social contract;' a tacit agreement between citizens and rulers, where the rulers are obliged to share their wealth to provide the individual citizen a comfortable and well-off lifestyle, while the role of the citizens is to exercise loyalty and political passivity in exchange for the provided neo-patrimonial benefits.[29] Herein lie the reason why these autocratic governments are not perceived as dictatorships by the citizens, but as 'benevolent monarchies' where the ruler acts in the best interest of his people (Fox, Mourtada-Sabbah, and al-Mutawa 2006a, 33ff). Cammett et al. (2015, 25) underscore this point by the observation that the cross-country experience in the Middle East region points out that the oil rich monarchies apply survival strategies in which they 'pacify' their population through wealth distribution, while oil countries with less income pr. capita, e.g., Algeria, Iran, and Iraq allocate oil rents only among their elites and invest in large repressive apparatuses.

RST has been, and still is, the all dominating theoretical lens through which social scientists have understood the economic and political dynamics of the Gulf states for the past three decades (Yalcin 2018), despite a growing critique (see e.g. Herb 1999; Hertog 2010; Luciani 2005; Gray 2011; Ulrichsen 2012, Section 1).[30] Particularly, scholars who study democratization and political representation processes are uncomfortable with the extent that RST continues to be used as an explanation for political passivity in the Gulf countries because it is plausible that the relationship between taxes and representation is far more complex than assumed in RST.[31] For example, Freer (2017) criticises RST for the failure to account for the existence of Islamist movements in rentier states.

Gray (2011) recognises that the RST retain a strong validity at the broader level but because of its static nature, RST has not been able to adequately explain the dramatic changes in the political economies seen in the Gulf during the past two decades. He argues that while RST has been well suited to explain the state-society relations in the Arab Gulf countries during the 1950-1980s, it has not been able to incorporate the

---

29 See e.g. Davidson (2005, 71ff) for account of the growth and content of the patrimonial networks and the social contract in UAE. Hertog (2014) uses the term the 'distributional bargain' synonymously with 'ruling bargain.'

30 See also the workshop preamble: *The Rentier State at 25: Dismissed, Revised, Upheld?* for the Fourth Gulf Research Meeting in Cambridge (Hertog and Luciani 2013).

31 This was one outcome of discussions held at a one day roundtable discussion sponsored by London School of Economics, 3 March 2016, on the topic of 'Establishing the Field of Gulf Studies: Reflection on Growth and Neglected Topics' with the participation of: Professor Toby Dodge, Dr. Courtney Freer, and Professor Steffen Hertog from LSE Middle East Centre; Professor Abdulkhaleq Abdulla, UAE University; Professor Martin Hvidt, Zayed University; Dr. Line Khatib, American University of Sharjah; Professor Gerd Nonneman, Georgetown University Qatar; Dr. Robert Stewart-Ingersoll, National Defense College Abu Dhabi; Dr. Marc Valeri, Exeter University; Dr. Karen Young, Arab Gulf States Institute Washington and LSE, and Dr. David B. Roberts, Kings College, London.

recent policy changes undertaken as a response to outside forces: globalization, new technology, free trade, investments regimes, social changes, and development imperatives. He suggests to introduce a dynamic element to the theory and argues for the inclusion of a 'third phase RST,' which recognises and explains the new type of Gulf Arabic states that are more responsive, globalised and strategic in its thinking, holds a stronger focus on state capitalist features and income earning capabilities and is considerably more responsive to new social pressures for reform and development than the earlier phases of RST (Gray 2011, 22ff). He argues that the limited role ascribed to rulers and governments in RST merely as distributors of oil wealth has proven wrong. By pointing to new research, among it, works done by me (Publication 3 and 4), Gray (2011) argues that the political elite does exercise agency and has developed a more nuanced, engaged and complex approach to society and to policy making, even if the fundamental reliance on rents continues to exist.

RST has been instrumental in conceptualization of the present research and I have found it academically fruitful to adopt and apply various elements of the RST in the analyses of the modern Gulf economies and their developmental trajectories. Foremost among them, Luciani's (1987) distinction between 'allocation states' and 'production states', which exposes fundamental differences between the two types of states and thus, facilitates a comparative approach with a sharp focus on the economic dynamics within the Gulf societies. Second, I have applied the concept of 'rentier mentality' in various studies (Publication 7) to explain and analyse the incentives the individual Gulf Arab or expatriate worker faces to be productive. In my interpretation, rentier mentality is closely related to the neoliberal concept of incentives both on an individual level and a societal level.

2.4.1.3 Distinct research topics

Social science-based Gulf studies took shape following the first oil crisis in 1973. The crisis spurred an academic interest into issues related to oil and gas, including petrodollar circulation and not least the inner working of the Gulf states. Scholarly and journalistic books related to the oil producing countries, in particular, Saudi Arabia and Kuwait, were published, bibliographies of the key actors, e.g., Sheikh Yamani, and institutions like OPEC, and the dominating oil companies nicknamed the 'Seven Sisters' remain a distinct feature of the Gulf studies (see e.g. Al-Kuwari 1978; Cause 1994; Crystal 1990; Field 1985; Kubursi 1984; Lacey 2009; Luciani 2005; Robison 1988; Yergin 1991, 2011).

Another set of research topics that are prominent in Gulf studies and, because of their specific regional focus distinguishes Gulf studies from Middle East studies, have been carried out mainly by political scientists in the academic field of international relations and security studies. The volatile situation in the Gulf, the importance of the region for the world economy both as an oil exporter and importer of finished products, and as an investor, the continuous conflict between Saudi Arabia and Iran concerning who should be the supreme power in the region, evolution of regional security agendas, the foreign policy and global rebalancing, and the spread of radical Islamism have featured prominently (see e.g. Aarts and Nonneman 2006, Ch. IV; Gause 1994; Gause 2010; Foley 2010; Sick 2009; Ulrichsen 2016b).

The third body of literature that I will argue distinguishes Gulf studies from Middle East studies is the academic interest in the inner workings of the Gulf region, spurred by the economic upturn commencing in the late 1990s with the rise in oil prices that continued to 2014, when oil prices fell sharply.[32] This body of studies, which could be labelled 'the economic, social, and political rise of the Gulf States', focuses on domestic issues and structures in the Gulf countries; on change and development, for example, changing domestic agendas in relation to political liberalization and participatory openings; on globalization; on gender issues; on labour market issues; on migrants' contribution/inclusion/exclusion; on social organization and development; on urban development and cityscapes; and on nationalism and national cohesion.

This category of studies concerned with the modern Gulf to which the present dissertation belongs, make up a very young field of study, basically gaining momentum after the year 2000. Some of the contributions are: Davidson (2005, 2006, 2009); El Katiri, Fattouh, and Paul (2012); Fox, Mourtada-Sabbah, and al-Mutawa (2006b); Gardner (2012); Henry and Springborg (2010, Ch. 6); Hertog (2014, 2010); Kamrava and Babar (2012); Kostiner (2000); Kropf (2016); Ménoret (2005, 2014); Ramakrishnan and Ilias (2011); Ulrichsen (2016a, 2017); Valeri (2009); Young (2014). Other important contributions to the study of the modern Gulf is the collection of research papers available from the Kuwait Programme on Development, Governance and Globalisation in the Gulf States published by London School of Economics and Politics.[33]

---

32 A small dent in the oil prices was recorded during the financial crisis 2009 and 2010.
33 Available at: http://www.lse.ac.uk/middleEastCentre/kuwait/publications/Research-papers.aspx

2 Situating the Dissertation within its intellectual framework

2.1.5 Conflicts and controversies within the field

The research field displays very little scholarly disagreement among the researchers. The social science oriented scholars all seem to be critical of the prevailing rentier state theory, but no 'schools' or distinct divisions have emerged within the field that provides a variation in theoretical perspectives or methodology. There is general agreement on the key concepts, e.g., social contract, oil rents, neopatrimonialism, and diversification. And furthermore, at the overall level there are no distinct clashes of evidence, and findings in the research output save differences resulting from analysis among the six Gulf countries. An outlier in this respect is Davidson (2012) who foresaw the collapse of the Gulf Monarchies in his book *After the Sheikhs*.

This overall lack of conflicts within this scholarly field does not come as a surprise. For as Yalcin (2018) points out, studies of politics and political economy in the Gulf region are "predominantly drawing upon modernization theory or rentier state theory," which links this field of study to the mainstream theoretical focus of (neo)liberalism.

However, there are researchers who approach the studies of the Gulf from a radical or Marxist perspective. Among them, Davis (2006) who in an article titled *Fear and Money in Dubai* published in New Left Review unravels the negative consequences of capitalist globalization; Kanna (2007) who in a MERIP publication titled *Dubai in a Jagged World* also focuses on the negative outcome of Dubai's capitalism, particularly in relation to the migrant labour force; and not least Hanieh's (2011) Marxist inspired class analysis published in his book *Capitalism and Class in the Gulf Arab States*.

However, despite few publications based on a radical perspective, and despite differences in interpretation of given findings, the overall picture is that a general consensus exists within this scholarly field.

This situation is most likely the outcome of the immaturity of the field which implies that so far the researchers have been occupied with the task of establishing data and thus, knowledge about the Gulf societies while serious attempts at theory building have been postponed until the scholarly field has achieved a higher level of insight into these societies. This is underscored by the particularistic approach generally applied by researchers in the field. A second likely reason for the apparent consensus and subdued debates within the field, might be a highly politicised research environment and the conscious or unconscious self-censorship exercised by researchers within the field.

2.1.6 Institutionalization of Gulf Studies

As mentioned, Gulf studies have only recently institutionalised themselves as a distinct scholarly field, with the advent of the Association for Gulf and Arabian Peninsula Studies (AGAPS) established in 2011.[34] The Mission Statement of AGAPS is:

> The Association for Gulf and Arabian Peninsula Studies (AGAPS) is a scholarly association. Its objectives are to promote high standards of scholarship and instruction, to facilitate collaboration between scholars, to encourage fieldwork and to mentor graduate students. AGAPS is multi-disciplinary and defines its area of study broadly to include the countries of the Arabian Peninsula, inclusive of the transnational flow of people, material and ideas across the Gulf, Red Sea and Indian Ocean.[35]

It is noteworthy that Iran and Iraq have been left out of the geographical definition, while Yemen is included. In this way, the geographical focus of the association is the group of countries normally referred to as the Gulf countries, the six member states of the Gulf Cooperation Council (GCC), i.e. Bahrain, Kuwait, Oman, Qatar, Saudi Arabia and the United Arab Emirates, and in addition, Yemen, which by some writers is considered the 7th GCC member (Al-Muslimi 2016). A second characteristic of Gulf studies as pointed out in the ASGAP mission statement is that they are multi-disciplinary, just like Middle East studies.[36]

---

34 In 2010 an informal meeting was held at the MESA conference in San Diego which resulted in the establishment of The Society for Gulf and Arabian Peninsula Studies (GAPS). The organization later changed name and was approved as an affiliated organization by MESA by July 2011.
35 See the AGAPS website: http://agaps.org/
36 An indication of the wide range of topics dealt with under the heading of Gulf studies is evident from the invitation to the Exeter Gulf conference July 2017 titled: Hegemonic Boundaries and Asymmetric Power in the Gulf. It included the following list of possible topics for papers: Gender, sex and identity; Race, ethnicity, purity, eugenics, biopower, anti-miscegenation; Class and alienation; Religious studies; Public sphere, political participation and citizenship; Temporal boundaries, age and 'youth'; Family, household and nation; Moral communities; Religion, sectarianism, Sunni-Shi'i counter-distinctions and dialectics; Rural and urban; Tribes and states; Resource management; Nationalism, citizenship, territory, sovereignty; Revolutionary and activist movements; Other practices and discourses; Liminality, liminal spaces; Legal issues and justice; Immigration, movement and belonging; Technology, social media, surveillance; Urban sociology, space and architecture; Archaeology, materiality, cartography and heritage; Political economy http://socialsciences.exeter.ac.uk/media/universityofexeter/instituteofarabandislamicstudies/centres/gulfstudies/conference/Exeter_Gulf_Conference_2017_-_Call_for_Papers.pdf

Scholars within Gulf studies generally publish in either the disciplinary journals or in the area studies journals associated with Middle East studies e.g. *International Journal of Middle East Studies, British Journal of Middle Eastern Studies* or *Middle Eastern Studies*. In 2011 an internationally-refereed scholarly journal focusing on the Arabian Peninsula and its surrounding waters was launched under the name: *Journal of Arabian Studies: Arabia, the Gulf, and the Red Sea* co-edited by Center for Gulf Studies at University of Exeter and School of Foreign Service in Qatar, Georgetown University, Qatar.

AGAPS is a relatively small association. By mid-2017, it had approximately 70 paying members with around 150 people on the list of past and current members. It is anticipated that the potential membership of the organization would be approximately 350 scholars.[37]

Research concerning the Gulf appears mainly to be carried out by individual researchers located in Middle East departments around the world. In addition to those, there are a good handful of institutions which focus on and thus facilitate Gulf research:

The Gulf/2000 Project was created in 1993 as a service to scholars, government officials, business people, journalists and other specialists who have a professional association with the Persian Gulf and Gulf studies.[38] They have organised 11 conferences, and to overcome data scarcity they have established two web-based services; a resource center or research collection and a network among scholars on the Gulf. Their level of activity has been diminishing lately due to lack of funding.[39]

The Centre for Gulf Studies at University of Exeter claim that it has the world's largest concentration of researchers in humanities and social sciences interested in the Gulf region, including the Arabian Peninsula, Iraq and Iran. They focus on a broad variety of issues related to the Gulf: archaeology, history, international relations, Islamic studies, material culture, political economy and politics. In addition, the Centre is hosting an annual Gulf conference, which celebrated its 30th anniversary in 2018.[40]

---

37 Mail correspondence with Victoria Hightower, secretary and membership coordinator at AGAPS, 1 September 2017.
38 http://gulf2000.columbia.edu/about.shtml
39 Discussion with Gulf/2000 Director for Research and Publications Lawrence Potter, at MESA Annual Meeting 2017, Marriott Wardman Park Hotel, Washington D.C., 20 November 2017.
40 https://socialsciences.exeter.ac.uk/iais/research/centres/gulf/

The Kuwait program at London School of Economics and Politics (LSE), or more formally titled The Kuwait Programme on Development, Governance and Globalisation in the Gulf States, has become a key contributor and powerhouse of Gulf research. In 2007, it was awarded a 10-year multi-disciplinary global programme funded by the Kuwait Foundation for the Advancement of Sciences (KFSA) and in May 2017, the funding was renewed for the period 2017-2022. So far, the programme that is based at the LSE Middle East Centre has commissioned more than 40 original research papers and has been instrumental in systematic and practical enquiry into fundamental questions in the social sciences of relevance to the Gulf.[41]

The Arab Gulf States Institute in Washington (AGSIW) was established in 2014, and is an independent, nonprofit institution that aims to increase the understanding and appreciation of the social, economic, and political diversity of the Arab Gulf states. "Through expert research, analysis, exchanges, and public discussion, the institute seeks to encourage debate and inform decision-makers shaping American policy regarding this region, deemed as having a critical geostrategic position." [42]

The Gulf Studies Programme, at the Centre for West Asian and African Studies of the School of International Studies, Jawaharlal Nehru University, New Delhi, India was established in March 1978. The center has a very distinct 'Gulf' focus and is predominantly social science-based. Main research areas are listed as: Reform process in the Gulf countries, Globalisation and Regionalism in the Gulf, Gulf Energy and Asian Regional Energy Cooperation, Gulf society in information Age, Indians in the Gulf. The number of faculty is six, and they teach both a Masters programme and a Doctoral programme.[43]

The Gulf Studies Programme, at the India Arab Cultural Centre at Jamia Millia Islamia, New Delhi, India. The center is staffed with three to four faculty and teaches a Masters programme in Arab-Islamic Culture and a Doctoral Programme in Gulf studies.[44]

Within the Gulf region itself there has been/is a few Gulf studies centers:

The *Gulf Research Center* (GRC), founded in 2000 by Dr. Abdulaziz Sager, a Saudi businessman, formerly based in Dubai, now based in Geneva and Jeddah. Besides research, the center disseminates political and

---

41 http://www.lse.ac.uk/middleEastCentre/kuwait/home.aspx
42 Website: http://www.agsiw.org/about/
43 Website: https://gspjnu.wordpress.com/about/
44 Website: http://jmi.ac.in/aboutjamia/centres/India-Arab-Cultural/courses-name/PhD-Gulf_Studies-496/1

economic news from the Gulf in both Arabic and English, and the Center organises the Gulf Research Meeting (GRM), an annual academic Gulf conference held in Cambridge UK, since 2010.

The *Gulf Studies Center* at Qatar University commenced operation in 2011. It encompasses the Gulf Studies Program which offers a Masters programme and a Ph.D programme in Gulf studies and the Gulf Studies Research Center, established in late 2013; which focuses on three areas: Energy and economics, Politics and Security and Social issues.[45]

The *Center for Gulf Studies*, American University of Kuwait, established 2012. It organises the so-called Gulf Studies Symposium, an international conference held biennially since 2013.[46]

2.1.7 Summary

The disciplinary roots of the scholarly field of Middle East studies are humanities and especially Philology and History. Despite the social science 'turn' of the field that commenced in the first decade after World War II, Philology and History continue to hold significant bearing on the discipline Of Middle East Studies (especially in a European context).

The scholarly field of Gulf studies recently emerged out of Middle East studies and thus carries on its key traits, among them, a humanistic orientation. However, the focus of this chapter was mainly on the social science-based Gulf studies, and it was argued that it distinguishes itself from Middle East studies on three parameters, the significant scarcity of data, its distinct theoretical basis, and its distinct set of research topics.

While historical and anthropological studies of the region and its people have been undertaken throughout the 19th and 20th century, social science-based studies are a relatively recent phenomenon. While studies related to both oil and to international relations have focused on the international markets and politics and thus could take advantage of international sources, the studies that deal with the domestic economy, politics, and social affairs are significantly hampered by a profound scarcity of relevant and accessible data sources, which inherently render it troublesome to conduct social science-based research.

---

45 Website: http://www.qu.edu.qa/artssciences/gulfstudies-center/about-us.php
46 http://www.auk.edu.kw/cgs/about_views_on_gulf.jsp

Hence, the scholarly field of Gulf studies does not only appear as a young field but also as immature because the academic knowledge of the societies under study is indeed limited. One implication of this is that theorization within the research field remains in its infancy.

Theoretically the field relies on rentier state theory that mostly appears as a collection of negative consequences related to the influx of large amounts of rents. It is static, lacks nuances and is unable to predict future behaviour. However, it still holds sway within Gulf studies to explain state-society relations.

This dissertation mirrors these constraints. It has been written as the field has defined itself and attempted to cope with its three distinguishing features. Hence, this dissertation both reflects these constraints, and at the same time it attempts to overcome them, pursuing the ultimate aim of contributing to the advancement of the field. However, the immaturity of the field has provided ample space for academic contributions.

2.2 Area Studies epistemology

The second element in the intellectual framework that forms the context of this dissertation is area studies, implying that this study is both conceived and carried out within the epistemological approach of area studies. This represents a deliberate choice of approach for this study and also reflects my academic upbringing within an area studies institution focusing on the Middle East.

Area studies - the organization of teaching and research along the lines of geographical and cultural regions (Mirsepassi, Basu, and Weaver 2003, 1) advocates and applies multi-disciplinary scholarship, because complex real-world problems rarely fall entirely within the purview of a single academic discipline. Furthermore, as pointed out by Tessler, Nachtwey, and Banda (1999, xiv) area studies represents a particularistic approach that especially in its earlier days was conceived to transcend ethnocentrism and Western bias and thus, to ensure accuracy and relevance of the research findings.

Szanton (2004, 4) provides the following generic definition of the concept of area studies as they developed in America after the Second World War:[47]

> Area studies is best understood as a cover term for a family of academic fields and activities joined by a commitment to: 1) intensive language study; 2) in-depth field research in the local language(s); 3) close attention to local histories, viewpoints, material, and interpretations; 4) testing, elabourating, critiquing, or developing grounded theory against detailed observations; and 5) multi-disciplinary conversations often crossing the boundaries of the social sciences and humanities.

Area studies, thus, represent an epistemological approach that differs markedly from that of the pure disciplines (e.g., politics, economy, anthropology, and sociology) i.e. that area studies emphasise particularistic or contextual knowledge as opposed to universal knowledge. The latter is advanced by using universally valid, scientific principles while the particularistic or contextual knowledge originates in the understanding that humanity and contexts are so fundamentally different that they demand separate study and representation (Ludden 2003, 131). Closely linked to this division between universalistic and particularistic approaches are the normative concepts of ideographic and nomothetic research (see e.g. Babbie 2013, 19-21).

While research, even the most universal of the social sciences and the most particularistic of the humanities disciplines ultimately depend on both type of knowledge (Ludden 2003, 131), the dichotomy between the two epistemological approaches are especially identifiable within the political science discipline.

Having a multi-disciplinary focus and being an area experts do not constitute a problem for the core humanistic disciplines like archaeolo-

---

[47] Area studies are not confined to the study of the Middle East but also to the former Soviet Union, East Asia, Latin America, Africa, South Asia, South East Asia, Eastern and Central Europe, and the three one-country area studies: China, Japan and Korea (Mirsepassi, Basu, and Weaver 2003, 2). In an European context, one should add a fourth one-country area study, namely American studies. Szanton, who himself was involved in financing the area studies in America through the Ford Foundation, finds that as each of the sub-fields of area studies developed over, they became neither internally homogeneous, nor similar to each other. In fact, they were strikingly distinctive in their political, institutional, and intellectual histories, and in their relationships with the disciplines (Szanton 2004, 4).

2.2 Area Studies epistemology

gy, history, philology, cultural and gender studies or Islamic studies. The same is true for the social science discipline of anthropology. In all these disciplines the researchers are by nature area experts, and as such have no problems being multi-disciplinary. The opposite is true for the discipline of economics.[48] Or stated differently, neither of these disciplines give the researcher the choice of being either an area expert or a theorist. The discipline of sociology traditionally focused its research on America and Western Europe, and thus did not aspire to be within area studies. However, political science, especially in America, understood as the disciplines of politics, International Relations (IR), and comparative politics had difficulties integrating themselves in the area studies concept due to a tension between regional specialists and discipline-oriented social scientists about how social science constructs knowledge. This tension manifests itself in the so-called area studies controversy in which discipline-oriented scholars accuse area studies scholars of being ideographic and particularistic, while the area studies scholars accuse the discipline oriented scholars of being nomothetic and universalistic (Tessler, Nachtwey, and Banda 1999, vii).[49]

There are several reasons why this controversy primarily became or is an American phenomenon. As Ludden (2003, 131ff) points out, area studies have been a feature of universities in Europe since the Enlightenment period and originate from an effort to support theories of human progress by comparing Europe to other regions of the world. While area studies have been a permanent feature of the university system in Europe, it was not introduced in America until the 1950s: First, as highlighted above, due to a near absence of area specialists, area studies centers within all regional areas were funded to support the new international role assumed by America after World War II. Second, and of more importance for this argument, as pointed out by Mitchell (2004, 84-5) there was a pronounced demand for multi-disciplinarity because, in contrast to the situation in Europe, by the 1950s the social disciplines in America had

---

48 However, the distinction is not so clear. Within economics the sub-disciplines, i.e. political economy and development economy continue to be far more applied sciences and thus closer to the area studies concept as will be evident in section 2.3. Within politics, some area specialists exist, within comparative politics and within sociology some area specialists can be found with the subfield, development sociology (Basedau and Köllner 2006, 25).
49 It is plausible that this controversy has manifested itself not only in terms of which conferences a scholar participates in or which journals he publishes in, but more fundamentally in allocation of research funding and, more importantly, in the formulation of job descriptions and thus eventually in who gets the academic positions.

divided themselves into highly discrete professional disciplines or areas of theoretical territories.

In a paragraph titled 'The Astonishing Growth of Area Studies', Szanton (2004, 5ff) points out that prior to World War II internationally-oriented teaching and research in America was extremely limited. No more than 60 PhDs about the contemporary non-western world had been written at American universities prior to 1940, and of these, most dealt with antiquity.[50] This situation is in sharp contrast to the early 2000s "where thousands of college and university faculty teach on the history, literature, contemporary affairs, and international relations of Africa, Asia, Latin America, The Middle East, and the former Soviet Union" (Szanton 2004, 6). Ford Foundation, the largest sponsor of the area studies centres, sponsored more than 5000 doctoral students and 2800 postdoctoral area studies projects from 1951 to 2002 (Szanton 2004, 10-1).

However, the support for area studies in the U.S. diminished during the early 1990s due to two related developments. The end of the Cold War, which left policymakers with less commitment to acquire area-based expertise, and second, the process of globalization (Mirsepassi, Basu, and Weaver 2003, 5; Tessler, Nachtwey, and Banda 1999, xiff). As Khalidi (2003, 183) polemically framed this point "there is no need to read their exotic languages or learn their strange customs in order to deal with them because they all will be speaking English and eating Big Macs soon, if they are not doing so already."

In America, the study of the Middle East was primarily institutionalised in area studies centres. At these centres, multi-disciplinarity was in focus. Traditionally trained Orientalists, with expertise in languages and culture, were expected to interact with scholars from other disciplines within the humanities. As a distinctively new feature to the field, they were also expected to interact with scholars from the social sciences disciplines, such as political scientists, economists, sociologist, and anthropologists.

Through this multi-disciplinary interaction, scholars could learn from each other and transcend the boundaries of their academic fields with the purpose of producing useful knowledge. The broader aim with the area studies philosophy was to create a new type of scholar that would master both the disciplinary traits related to theories and methodology, while at the same time hold an extensive empirical knowledge. Ward (1975) explained it this way, 'the new scholar' should process 'two skills in

---

50   See also Lockman (2010, 122-3).

one skull' (Ward, 1975 cf. Valbjørn 2008, 67). But as pointed out by Tessler, Nachtwey, and Banda (1999, x) this ideal situation was never attained as it seems like disciplined oriented social scientist and area specialist continue to "inhabit two different scholarly worlds" as they generally do not read or publish in the same journals or attend the same conferences.

As mentioned above, in Europe area studies took on quite a different form, generally as a much more integrated part of the academic landscape and thus, the so-called controversy only plays as marginal role in a European context (for an overview of Area Studies in Europe see e.g. Basedau and Köllner 2006; Schäbler 2007; Valbjørn 2009, 2008).

Eckert (2005: 46-47) argues that in Germany, and in Europe in general, three distinct strands can be discerned in area studies, "namely (1) a classical or philological strand which focuses on the specifics of the language, literature, arts, and (pre-modern) history of a given region, (2) a social science strand which includes political science plus some branches of economics, sociology, and human geography, and (3) a culture studies strand which brings together some of the region-oriented work in sociology, ethnology, anthropology, the humanities, and newer inter-disciplinary study clusters such as gender studies, film and media studies, ethnic studies, etc." (Eckert 2005: 46-47 cf. Basedau and Köllner 2006, 19-20).

Centre for Contemporary Middle East studies at the University of Southern Denmark, where I have worked for a quarter of a century, fits the description of the second strand. The centre was established in 1983 with the purpose of providing applied knowledge concerning the Middle East not only to students but also to public authorities, the business community and to the general public. The focus of the centre was the contemporary Middle East (defined as the 20th century primarily after World War II) and the naming of the centre represented an explicit attempt to distance itself from the classic philological strands dominating the study of the Middle East in Denmark at the time.[51] The centre is nested within the Department of History that also includes other Area studies.[52]

The Centre for Contemporary Middle East studies resembles the American type area studies centre with its focus on useable knowledge brought forward by an interdisciplinary staffing that represents a mixture of social science, humanities, and applied Arabic language. Over the

---

51 For an overview of Orientalism in Denmark, see the various contributions in Rump (2006). See also Valbjørn and Andersen (2005).
52 Center for American Studies, Centre for Medieval Studies, Centre for Cold War Studies, Danish Centre for Welfare Studies, Centre for Maritime and Business History and Centre for Medieval and Renaissance Studies.

years, and especially since the University declared the field of modern Middle East studies a priority research area within the Faculty of Humanities at University of Southern Denmark in 2007, the center has decreased its focus on the production of applied and thus immediately usable knowledge, and has placed a stronger emphasis on purely academic outputs and more discipline-oriented research (Jung 2016).[53]

Valbjørn (2008, 67-70) categorises this centre as 'area studies lite', meaning that the centre closely resembles the American type area studies but differ in two respects, i.e. that its focus is limited to the modern Middle East and that the staff consists of "a *single* geographer, economist, sociologist, political scientist, religious historian, and a few historians and Arab linguists united by a common interest in contemporary affairs in a specific geographic area." The implication of the latter is that while the centre provides a critical mass of colleagues who share the interest in the geographical region, this centre, like other 'area studies lite' centres suffers from a lack of critical mass of colleagues within each scholarly discipline. That implies a lack of a common language in terms of approaches or methodologies and renders it less possible that a cross fertilization of ideas and approaches takes place within the centre. To mitigate this problem at the Centre for Contemporary Middle East studies, we have emphasised that each researcher establishes discipline-oriented professional connections to their respective academic fields, e.g., through research collabouration, scholarly exchange programmes, and participation in professional events.

2.2.1 Summary

This dissertation is highly influenced by the area studies epistemology, implying that it is multi-disciplinary, has a particularistic touch to it, as it favours an empirical and contextual foundation as the basis for solid theory formation, and not least holds a focus on contemporary and policy relevant content.

According to multi-disciplinarity, the individual studies included in this dissertation are shaped by and build on theories and middle-range theories primarily from the disciplines of economics/development economics, geography – in itself an interdisciplinary field – and political science, which will be discussed in more detail in the next section.

---

53   For further information about Centre for Contemporary Middle East Studies, see Jung (2016); Nielsen (1997, 2006); Mørch (1996).

Area studies epistemology is underpinned – or in my view necessitated - by the immaturity of the research field of Gulf studies. As argued above, the near absence of social science-related data, poses – and continues to pose – significant problems to research and is likely to preclude strictly disciplinary studies. As argued by Mitchell (2004, 84), whereas it is possible in highly developed countries, e.g., Europe or America to divide social analysis into sharply distinct fields, e.g., of economy, politics, culture, and society, this is not the case for the study of "backward regions of the non-West."

In the Gulf context, this certainly appears true, not only due to the data deficiencies, but more fundamentally because the societal reality in the Gulf states constitute a difficult decipherable mixture of formal governance system (as represented by Sheikhs, the ruling families, and the elites) superposed by kinship and tribal structures, and not least strong religious sentiments. Thus, in my view, this societal reality renders it impossible to draw a meaningful distinction between politics, economy, and culture. Hence, a multi-disciplinary and particularistic approach has been deemed necessary for my research.

This viewpoint is elegantly echoed by Samin (2017, 526) who in a recent roundtable on the challenges of doing fieldwork in the Middle East published by the *International Journal of Middle East* illustrates the need for a multi-disciplinary academic approach in the study of the Arab Gulf countries. He writes:

> Few modern states defy the reigning scholarly consensuses of economics, politics, history, and anthropology like Saudi Arabia, a place that on account of oil wealth has been transformed almost beyond recognition in the span of two or three generations. As a rentier-based, kinship-organised, orally inscribed, puritanically orthodox Muslim polity, Saudi Arabia poses problems for the best tradition of graduate training in any single discipline. [...] To be a successful researcher in Saudi Arabia demands rigorous interdisciplinarity. Acquiring fluency with the kingdom's three distinguishing features – its rentier political economy, its Wahhabi religious culture, and its kinship and oral traditions – requires that one be equal parts political scientist, historian, and anthropologist. Due to the immaturity of the research field and the complex societal realities surrounding the subject field addressed in each of the individual studies which make up this dissertation, a natural first step has been to map 'what is out there' in a multi-disciplinary and particularistic fashion, in order for the research to become part of a cumulative knowledge formation process that ultimately can make way for theorization.

2.3 Development Economics

The third element of the intellectual framework forming this dissertation is the academic field of development economics. Development economics largely defines the subject field of the enquiry, implying an explicit focus on societal development, the underlying (neo)-classical conception of economic behavior, the specific topics of the enquiry addressed in the individual studies, and the middle-range theories applied.

Development economics as it is known today is both a mono- and multi-disciplinary social science discipline emerging in the aftermath of the Second World War, due in large parts to the developmental challenges that followed the decolonialization of the Third World countries.[54] It first emerged as a specific perspective within the field of economics and later as a sub-discipline (Martinussen 2005, 19) that dealt with the "kinds of policies that an active state and the international community could adopt to accelerate a country's rate of development" (Meier and Rauch 2005, 73).[55]

During the first decades after the Second World War, development research was predominantly conceived of as an economic matter manifested in a focus on economic growth and economic transformation. Economic models that had worked for North-Western countries were transferred with little or no modification to the developing countries as a part of the 'modernization' thinking. However, starting in the mid-1970s

---

54 See Meier and Rauch (2005, 73-8) for a succinct analysis of the evolution and characteristics of the discipline of Development Economics.
A substantial body of studies and literature reviews dealing with this academic field have been published over the last half century. Among them, the following, which have formed the background for this study. The more than one thousand pages long *Handbook of Development Economics*, now in its 5th version edited by Rodrik and Rosenzweig (2009b), the book, *Society, State & Market A guide to competing theories of Development* (Martinussen 2005); the 87 pages review article *The Economics of Development: A survey* (Stern 1989) and not least the overview of the field provided in highly qualified and long established textbooks e.g. *Leading Issues in Economic Development* (8th edition) by Meier and Rauch (2005); *Economic Development* (12th edition) by Todaro and Smith (2015) or *Growth & Development: With Special Reference to Developing Economies* (8th edition) by Thirlwall (2006) and *Economic Growth* (3rd edition) by Weil (2016).
The aim of this section is not to provide a comprehensive study of the field of development economics and thus, there is no pretence of being exhaustive. Please refer to the literature above for such a review. The purpose is rather to point to those aspects of this research that have had a bearing on my research approach.
55 Debates have been going on within the scholarly field of economics about whether or not there should be a separate field of development economics: In Lewis' presidential address to the *American Economic Association* in December 1983, titled "The State of Development Theory", he argues that the contextual and structural differences between the developed and developing economies warrant a distinct discipline of development economics (Lewis 1984). As he states "The overlap between Development

development research broadened its scope beyond pure economics, as politics and culture were incorporated into the research field with the aim of increasing its explanatory value "as researchers, politicians, and planners consistently tried to reach a broader and deeper understanding of the problems facing developing countries" (Martinussen 2005, 5).[56]

With the incorporation of the academic fields of politics and culture, development economics turned into the broader scholarly field of development studies. This field increasingly paid attention to non-economic conditions for growth and development, i.e. increased focus on the specific context in each country, to social and cultural differentiation, people-centered development, gender and ecological conditions, etc. However, development economics has been maintained as a distinct scholarly discipline (see e.g. Thirlwall 2006; Meier and Rauch 2005; Stern 1989).

In his extensive review of the competing theories of development, Martinussen (2005, 18ff) argues that the field of development economics remains distinct within the field of development studies, due to the fact that the intellectual origin of development economics differs from the sociological and political science approaches, which underpin the cultural and political side. He identifies the theoretical origins of development economics in works by Smith, Malthus, Ricardo, Keynes, and Schumpeter.

At the general level, the academic field of development economics has – along with other social science disciplines – experienced three major epochs or intellectual shifts since the Second World War. First, as mentioned, *modernization theory*, which dominated developmental studies from the 1940s into the 1970s. It is founded on classical economy thinking and held the basic claim that all societies progress through similar stages of development. Thus, development was viewed as a process of modernization, in which the Third World countries developed (politically and economically) towards greater similarity with the North-Western World (Martinussen 2005, 38). A primary example of modernization theory was Rostow's stage of growth theory in which the development process is depicted as an aircraft taking off. The driver behind development, i.e. what increases its speed and finally facilitates the take-off toward maturity, is mainly reduced to one factor, investments (Rostow 1960).

Economics and the Economics of the Developed is bound to be great [...] However, the differences are also rather large, which is why each also has some tools of its own" (Lewis 1984, 2).

56 See also the overview by Rodrik and Rosenzweig (2009a) of the advances within the field in their introduction to the 5th edition of the *Handbook of Development Economics*.

The second epoch was the *dependencia* school and the new left, which gained influence in the late 1960s or early 1970s and impacted social sciences for about a decade. The approach was Neo-Marxist and criticised the notion embedded in modernization theory, that all countries will pass through similar stages of development as the developed countries had done. The central tenet of dependency theory was that the capitalistic nature of the world market would exploit countries in the 'periphery' and transferred wealth to the 'core' countries. In other words, the structure of the world system systematically kept the developing countries in a stage of underdevelopment. The school was founded on the basic understanding embedded in the Prebish-Singer thesis, developed in the late 1940s, which argued that exporters of primary products (e.g. coal, cotton, cereals) will face deteriorating terms-of-trade in relation to countries exporting manufactured goods (e.g., cars, washing machines, computers). More specifically, Andre Gunder Frank (1966) argued how development and underdevelopment could and did coexist in the world economy. Samir Amin (1974) analysed the structural mechanisms of the exploitation and Immanuel Wallerstein used a life time to conduct the so-called World Systems Analysis.

The third intellectual shift within development economics was so manifest or encompassing that Gore (2000) denotes it a paradigmatic shift. It was the return to neoliberal economics colloquially known as *Washington consensus* within development economics. However, this shift was much wider in scope and was spearheaded by political heads of state, notably President Ronald Reagan, Prime Minister Margaret Thatcher and Chancellor Helmut Kohl in the 1980s and was further strengthed by the fall of the Berlin wall and the collapse of the Soviet Union, which meant an end to the Cold war (Williamson 2003). Todaro and Smith (2011, 126ff) apply the term 'The Neoclassical Counterrevolution' to denote the manifest return to market fundamentalism, which was implied in this intellectual shift. The basic claim embodied in neoliberal economics is that the market by itself will allocate resources efficiently, and that the state should only interfere in the economy to keep the 'playing field level' for the actors in the market. Whereas both modernization theorists and writers from the dependency school would point to 'market failure' as a key reason for lack of developmental results, neoliberal writers would generally point to 'government failure.' [57] In a theoretical perspective,

---

57 See Lockman (2010, Chpt. 5) for an account of how each of the three intellectual shifts has impacted Oriental studies/Middle East studies. Note especially, how he (p. 134) finds significant similarities between Orientalism and Modernization theory.

neoliberal economy implies that all societies and markets are believed to operate on the same set of universal economic laws. As such, all societies are fundamentally identical and thus can be analysed with the same methods and tools.

The neoliberal economic approach was implemented – among other institutions – through the International Financial Institutions most prominently by the International Monetary Fund (IMF) and the World Bank. In this way, the approach directly impacted the developing countries both through the direct conditions attached to the lending, and also indirectly by the assessment of the soundness of each country's economic policies and performances made by these institutions, most notably the Article IV consultations carried out by IMF (see Publication 1).

However, the very strict adherence to 'market fundamentalism' in the 1980s has been relaxed somewhat over time so that contexts, institutions, and not least the state have returned to a more prominent role. This transformation within the neo-liberal approach has been explicated in the shift from 'Washington consensus' to 'Santiago consensus' announced in 1997 by the then President of the World Bank (Wolfensohn 1998). See e.g., Stiglitz (2002) for a substantiated critique of the neoliberal approach as it was played out by the International Financial Institutions in relation to development and globalization.

This dissertation has been written during the time period where the paradigm of neoliberal economy has been hegemonic. This has influenced the topical focus of the dissertation, e.g., the context of globalization, the focus on incentives, and not least the direct focus on economic reforms. However, the level of concentration of public wealth, state dirigism, and neo-patrimonial ties found in the UAE and the Gulf more generally, as documented throughout my studies, have certainly challenged the usefulness of the strict neoliberal approach in the studies of the Gulf states.

Throughout this research, I have defined development as "a multidimensional process involving major changes in social structures, popular attitudes, and national institutions as well as the acceleration of economic growth, the reduction of inequality, and the eradication of poverty" (Todaro and Smith 2011, 16). Furthermore, they define the academic discipline of development economics as "the economic, social, political, and institutional mechanisms, both public and private, necessary to bring about rapid (at least by historical standards) and large-scale improvements in standard of living for the peoples of Africa, Asia, Latin America, and the formerly socialist transition economies" (Todaro and Smith 2011, 8).

While the latter definition is indeed broad and encompassing, it delineates the field in important ways. Development economics deals with society and societal issues. In other words, it is conceived within the discipline of social sciences, and thus, leaves natural sciences, health and engineering outside of the research field, to the extent, where they do not directly interact and influence the standard of living.

A notable feature of these definitions is that they allocate a prominent role to institutions. In my studies, institutions are defined as "humanly devised constraints that structure political, economic and social interaction" (North 1991, 97). Economists generally associate institutions such as property rights, political stability, dependable legal system, honest governments, and competitive and open markets with factors facilitating growth.

Following the intellectual plea to 'bring the state back in' to the analysis of politics (Evans, Rueschemeyer, and Skocpol 1985) there has been an 'institutional turn' within the social sciences (Evans 2005; Waldner 1999, 5). As pointed out by North (1991, 97), institutions play a vital role in economic development.

> Together with the standard constraints of economics they [institutions] define the choice set and therefore determine transaction and production costs and hence the profitability and feasibility of engaging in economic activity. They evolve incrementally, connecting the past with the present and the future; history in consequence is largely a story of institutional evolution in which the historical performance of economies can only be understood as a part of a sequential story. Institutions provide the incentive structure of an economy; as that structure evolves, it shapes the direction of economic change towards growth, stagnation, or decline.

Institutions and institutional analyses are central to this dissertation both conceptually and in a more specific way through application of the approach of historical institutionalism (see e.g. Hall and Taylor 1996; Peters, Pierre, and King 2005). This approach divides history into 'critical junctures' and periods of stability termed 'path-dependence' (North 1990, 92ff; Amenta 2012, 50ff). In several of the studies that form this dissertation, I have explicitly used this framework to conceptualise the analyses of the historical evolution and retention of e.g., the business-friendly climate permeating Dubai, which contrasts greatly the climate elsewhere in the region (Publication 2), or in my analyses of the profound societal changes triggered by the sudden influx of vast amounts of oil money (Publications 3, 5, 6, 7).

To further delineate the discipline of development economics the table below provides a comparison between development economics and the two major disciplines within economics, i.e. neo-classical economics and neo-marxist economics.

Table 1. Comparison of different theoretical approaches

Approaches	Unit of analysis		Scope of valitidy		Analytical perspective	
	Individual actor	Structures	Monoeconomics	Plurality of Economics	Monodisciplinary	Multidisciplinary
Neo-classical Economics	**		**		**	
Development Economics	*	**		**	**	*
Neo-Marxist Political economy		**		**		**

Note: Two asterisks indicate where the emphasis of the three major approaches lies. In the case of development Economics, one asterisk indicates a further area of secondary importance. Source: Martinussen (2005, 54)

The three economic approaches differ in unit of analysis, scope of validity, and analytical perspective. In contrast to neo-classical economics, development economics primarily focuses on the macro-economic structures in societies and not the individual. The discipline of development economics views economies in specific contexts and thus operate with a plurality of economic systems. And finally, while development economics does apply both mono-disciplinary and multi-disciplinary approaches, the general preference is for the former.

Both development economics and neo-marxist economy distance themselves from neo-classical economics as they both operate with an interlinkage between politics and economics as embodied in the term political economy.[58] Furthermore, in contrast to Neo-classical and Neo-Marxists, development economists tend to view industrialised and developing economies as qualitatively different entities, implying the application of different methods and theories in the analysis of the two categories of entities.

---

58 As pointed out by Stern (1989, 617), the term 'political economy' is vaguely defined, but encompasses how any "suggested policy is likely to be received, manipulated, obstructed or supported" by various groups in society.

The scholarly discipline of development economics also distinguishes itself from other disciplines of economy by the emphasis it places on certain specific research topics. Thirlwall (2006, 8) polemically delineates the research field by stating that "Development Economics is what development economists do." In his lengthy review of the scholarly field, Stern (1989, 669) identifies what he labels 'the grand issues' of the subject field, i.e. (i) the role of the state (ii) the process of growth and change (iii) the influence of industrialization and trade (iv) the relations between developed and developing countries (v) structural adjustment and stabilization (vi) population and the economy (vii) the objectives of development and strategies for achieving them." [59] As pointed out by Stern (1989), none of these topics or issues are unique to development economics, but what distinguishes development economics from other branches of the academic field of economics is that these issues have been central to the discipline, and that major theoretical contributions have resulted from this research on development.[60]

A final feature that distinguishes development economics from the broader field of economics is its applied focus. The field of development economics was so to speak 'born' with an applied focus, i.e. to advice the newly decolonised countries how to attain growth and development. Hence, there has been close relationship between the worlds of research and practice (Rodrik and Rosenzweig 2009a, xvi). One outcome of this relationship is that the research agenda of development economics has been influenced by the changing political priorities in international development co-operation. Shifting sectoral focus, e.g., on industrialization; rural development; people's participation; transnational corporations; or the shifts in general strategies, e.g., meeting 'Basic Human Needs'; developing country debt; green revolution; fair trade; private sector aid; women in development; development and security; poverty alleviation; aid and the environment and the latest combined efforts, the Millennium Development Goals (MDG's) and the new Sustainable Development Goals (SDG's).

---

59 These grand themes closely resemble the 'broad policy themes' which Meier and Rauch (2005, 78) highlight as the emphasis of traditional development economics: 1) industrialization, 2) rapid capital accumulation, 3) mobilization of underemployed manpower, and 4) planning and an economically active state.
 The list of grand issues is vindicated by the contents of standard text books within Development Economics e.g. (Todaro and Smith 2011; Meier and Rauch 2005) and (Thirlwall 2006).
60 See Lewis (1984, 3) for list of models which are the outcome of the theoretical work of development economists.

These changing emphases related to development goals and strategies have led to a degree of fragmentation of the research field into disparate and unrelated theoretical propositions concerning specific societies. According to Martinussen (2005, 353-4), this has impacted the nomothetic efforts within the field negatively in relation to identification of general trends and patterns of correlations. He goes as far as to point to "fashion' trends in theory construction and in areas of focus."

2.3.1 Growth Models

Development economics as a discipline includes a conceptualization of the mechanisms and processes creating growth and development. The field operates with three fundamental components in growth processes: 1) capital accumulation, 2) growth in population and its qualifications, and 3) technological progress (Weil 2009, Part I and II).

Economists have attempted to specify the relationship among these factors through modeling. The overall aim has been to understand the causes of long term growth, and in -growth variation, that is, why some countries experience higher growth rates than others.

The component of technological progress has played a particularly perplexing role in this modeling. The neo-classical models notably the Harrod-Domar model (1936 and 1946) and its modified version the Solow model (1956) have been the centrepiece of modern growth theory until the 1980s (Jones and Manuelli 2005, 17). Both models emphasise capital as the limiting factor in growth and thus place a focus on domestic savings in the development process.[61] Furthermore, both models leave technological progress unexplained. Technology is treated as an exogenous variable, implying that advance in technology and the productivity enhancing effects it has, is viewed as outside the control of the individual economies. The so-called 'Solow residual' indicated that nearly 50% of observed historical growth in industrialised countries is stemming from technological progress, and as such is left unexplained in the models (Todaro and Smith 2011, 150).

Endogenous growth theory or new growth theory as it is also termed, was developed in the mid-1980s to better explain observed growth. New growth theory is associated with the work of Paul Romer (1986) and Rob-

---

[61] For a comprehensive account of the development of the neoclassical and endogenous growth models, see Aghion and Howitt (2009, Chapt. 1 and 2). See Jones and Manuelli (2005), for a detailed account of the AK growth model.

ert Lucas (1988) and basically argues that innovation and the advent of new technologies do not happen by chance, but that both factors can be created by investments in knowledge, research and development of products, and in human capital. In other words, policies and investments can create growth in the 'knowledge capital' which they believe have significant spillover effects on the economies. In this way, technology becomes an endogenous factor of growth.

An additional element of new growth theory is that it assumes that the marginal product of capital is constant or increasing rather than diminishing as it is assumed to be in the neoclassical theories of growth. The implication is that in new growth theory, long term sustained growth is possible, a result not possible in neo-classical theory due to the assumption of diminishing returns to scale.

New growth theory thus has clear policy implications, i.e. that the long run growth rates of an economy depend on policy measures. Governments can promote growth by providing incentives to agents in the knowledge-producing, human-capital-intensive sector (Meier and Rauch 2005, 79). So, in addition to a continued emphasis on savings and investment for long term growth, new growth theory places governmental policies at the center of the growth process through investments in human capital, innovation, and knowledge building. As is evident from the development trajectories pursued in the Arab Gulf states, the governments in the region are highly influenced by this nexus between enhancement of human capital and growth.

2.3.2 Summary

According to Martinussen (2005, 353), development economics has not succeeded in devising overall theories or models of growth and development applicable to all Third World countries. The theoretical contributions of development economics are characterised by middle-level theory building, which focuses on phenomena between structures and individual actors.

Development economics as a scholarly field has made four significant impressions on the research conducted in this dissertation: First, it offers a unique focus to my studies, i.e. that of development and transition. For example, in this dissertation I have been less concerned with economic diversification, state reforms, or improvement in human capital *per se*, but focused on how each of these factors contribute to the long-term growth and development of the Gulf societies. This perspective implies that effects or outcomes of the analyses are assessed in relation to the potential impact on growth and development.

Second, development economics implies a focus on society. The unit of analysis is society at large, not the individual citizen, the company, or the sector.

Third, societal development takes time, which means that effects of policy initiatives undertaken today might first show in the medium or long term. In a Braudelish way, development thus implies a focus in which day-to-day politics is substituted with a focus on longer-term perspectives related to more consistent features of society, e.g., building competitiveness or preparing the next generation of citizens to become active knowledge workers. Furthermore, this approach is underpinned by the institutional focus throughout my writings.

Fourth, the academic field of development economics has provided the overall economic approach and not least the various mid-level theories that I have applied through my various analyses such as Hirschman's ([1958] 1969) notion of Forward and Backward linkages in spurring industrial growth; Kuznet's (1967, 1973) work on structural transformation; Porter's (1998) work on industrial clusters; Rosenstein-Rodan's (1943) 'Big push' resulting from concerted investments; Schumpeter's (1961) entrepreneurs and the resulting 'creative destruction', and more broadly, developmental state theory which follows the intellectual contributions of writers such as Polany ([1944] 2001), Gerschenkron ([1962] 1966) and Evans (1989, 1995).

2.4 Chapter summary

The aim of this dissertation is to advance science within the scholarly field of Gulf studies, through studies of the developmental trajectory of the Arab Gulf states. This chapter has reviewed the scholarly field of Gulf studies in its historical, institutional, and theoretical aspects.

While the disciplinary roots of Middle East studies and later Gulf studies are history, philology and to some extent anthropology, the focus of this review has mainly been on the social science aspects of the discipline, because it is of special relevance for this dissertation. It was argued that the field distinguishes itself from Middle East studies in three important ways: the significant scarcity of data, its distinct theoretical basis, and its distinct set of research topics. The data scarcity has been - and continues to be – a significant hurdle to further advancement of the field and its theoretical underpinning. Lack of data leads to lack of knowledge and thus, hampers theory formation. Hence, it can be claimed, that not only is the field young but also immature. Rentier state theory continues to dominate the field, despite significant criticism. This dissertation challenges rentier state theory on several points.

Secondly, the epistemological approach pursued was analysed and explicated with a point of origin in the area studies approach. This approach, which dominates scholarly work within the field of Gulf studies emphasises multi-disciplinarity, value contextual (or particularistic) knowledge, and has less of a nomothetic aim than the pure disciplines. It was argued that this approach was necessitated by – among other things – the societal reality in the Gulf states, which constitutes a difficult decipherable mixture of formal governance systems, superposed by kinship and tribal structures, and not least, strong religious sentiments. This societal reality renders it impossible to draw a meaningful distinction between politics, economy, and culture. Hence, a multi-disciplinary and particularistic approach has been deemed both necessary and appropriate for the studies carried out within this dissertation.

The third element in the intellectual framework was the scholarly field of development economics. Development economics largely defined the subject field of the enquiry, which includes the focus on development, on societies, on long term structural change, and of the economic approaches. Among them, the underlying neo-classical conception of economic behavior and growth, the specific topics of the enquiry addressed in the individual studies, and the middle-range theories applied.

3. Development in the Gulf states – Presentation of the enclosed articles and outline of key findings

The study of the developmental trajectory in the Arab Gulf states undertaken in this dissertation has been carried out through a series of scholarly publications each with (a) specific topic(s) and research question(s) and also with variations in the theory and methodology applied. Theoretically, the studies span from rentier state theory, developmental state theory, historical institutionalism, to more general growth theory. The sources used encompass interviews, academic literature, statistical reference works, national plans, and 'grey' papers, e.g., magazines and news articles. The methodology applied encompass qualitative interviews, critical text reading, content analysis, data analysis, data triangulation, and the topical focus in the selected publications cover a display of the 'grand themes' within development economics, i.e. state models and roles, state-led development, planning, diversification, industrialization and service sector development, knowledge economy, migration and its contribution to growth and development, economic clusters and competitiveness, and politics and political structures.

Below, the nine publications included in this dissertation will be presented and their contribution to the scholarly field of Gulf studies will be outlined. The publications are presented in chronological order, i.e. according to publication date as they reflect a steep learning curve for me as a researcher concerning the Gulf countries and the specific developmental issues which arise. Furthermore, as argued above the scholarly field of 'Gulf studies' has undergone significant advancement during the decade and a half through which the articles were researched and written, resulting in increased knowledge formation, slightly improved access to data and a higher level of institutionalization. In other words, the intellectual inquiries and outcomes in the enclosed publications are developed in dialogue not only with the field's constraints and challenges but also with its empirical and theoretical insights.

Below, I present a brief overview of each article, in which I explicate the intellectual motivation behind each study, the research question(s), the findings, and the contribution the study has made to the scholarly field of Gulf studies.

I recognise that my account of the scholarly contribution(s) embodied in this dissertation might appear self-promoting and lacking academic modesty, when for example I claim to be the first to have introduced a theory or a data source, or a special focus, e.g., on planning into Gulf studies. In mature scholarly fields, this would rarely happen, but not so in the nascent field of Gulf studies. First, as argued throughout the dissertation, the field of Gulf studies was, and still is, both very young and immature, thus leaving many 'firsts' or 'news' to the scholars initially involved. Second, my academic background in geography, a discipline that emphasises physical and economic planning, and as a development economist gives me a research focus, which was – and is – rare within the field of Gulf studies. As the field of Gulf studies has been dominated by scholars from the disciplines of history, and to a lesser extent anthropology and political science, the issues related to planning and development economics have largely fallen outside the specific scope of these scholarly groups, providing opportunity – and encouragement – for me, to venture into uncharted territory.[62]

---

[62] Today a handful of geographers can be found in the field of Gulf studies. They are mainly German scholars and focus broadly on urbanism, urban space, logistics, tourism and migration. E.g. Steffen Wipple, Zentrum für Nah-und Mittelost-Studien, Philipps Universität Marburg, Nadie Scharfenort and Ala Al-Hamarneh both at Geographisches Institut, Johannes Gutenberg-Universität Mainz (D), Christian Steiner, Mathematisch-Geographische Fakultät der Katholischen Universität Eichstätt-Ingolstadt, and Brigitte Dumortier, a French geographer formerly employed at NYU Abu Dhabi.

Publication 1

Hvidt, Martin. 2004. "Limited Success of the IMF and the World Bank in Middle Eastern Reforms." Journal of Social Affairs. 21 (81): p. 77-103.

In contrast to the other publications enclosed in this dissertation, the geographic focus of this article is the entire MENA region. The paper grew out of an emerging academic understanding by the late 1990s and early 2000s that the MENA countries – as a region – in a comparative perspective had fared badly, economically, over the preceding decade and a half. The region had not kept up with international growth rates and economic achievements, even when compared to other developing countries. Hence, the wider prospects for providing jobs and a decent livelihood for the region's rapidly increasing populations looked bleak, possibly leading to "serious consequences for political stability" (Henry and Springborg 2001, 2). This point was vindicated by the 'Arab Uprising' occurring approximately a decade later.

Following the turn to the Washington Consensus paradigm with its strong neo-liberal conviction and focus on macro-economic stability, open economies, privatization, and deregulation in the 1980s the International Financial Institutions (IFIs) had assumed a significant role globally but especially in – or – toward the developing countries. One of the prime focusses of the Washington Consensus paradigm was to replace the state-led, inward-oriented import-substitution-policies, which the IFIs themselves had been advocating during the 1950-1970s as a vehicle of growth, with free market policies to promote domestic industrial production in the developing countries.

The point of departure was the poor economic performance and the obvious – as claimed by neo-liberalists – need for serious economic reforms in the MENA countries. On that background, the paper raises the question why the IMF and the World Bank did not seem to facilitate serious reforms in, what increasingly had come to be understood as, dysfunctional economic policies, based on neo-patrimonial patron-client relations, crony capitalism, etc. Stated more precisely, why did these institutions only seem to have a modest success in engaging the region in a structural reform process?

This study finds that the impact of IMF and the World Bank in the MENA region is indeed limited, due primarily to low levels of lending but probably just as important, from active resistance by elite groups to outside intervention. The article hypothesises that three underlying reasons have made it possible for the politicians in the region to sidestep demands from the international – and national – society: The colonial legacy, the magnitude of strategic rent, and the prevalence and depth of state dominance in the production sector.

Thus, this paper documents that the IFIs which colloquially are said to play the role of the frontrunners for neo-liberalism and globalization, particularly in the developing world, did not have much leverage in the MENA region. First, due to the limited loan amounts, which translate into little leverage; second, due to the socio-political systems in the region, which effectively resisted their influence. The prevalence of strategic rents and remittances largely obscured the impact of unsustainable economic policies, and the existing elites had been able to hold on to their privileged position that largely had blocked the advent of neo-liberal free market principles.

The contribution of this paper to the scholarly field of Gulf studies, is to document the limited leverage the IFIs are holding in the MENA region. This is especially true for the capital rich Gulf states. The implication of this finding is that the decision either to abstain from pursuing economic reforms or to implement them, primarily rests with the decision-makers in each country. In other words, this finding suggests that the research field should focus primarily on the domestic or internal factors in each country, if the aim is to analyse and explain the adoption or non-adoption of economic reforms.

Publication 2

Hvidt, Martin. 2007. "Public – private ties and their contribution to development. The case of Dubai." *Middle Eastern Studies*. 43 (4): p. 557-577.

This paper is the first in a trilogy that set out to explore the developmental trajectory of Dubai. The article reads as an historical account of the development of Dubai and aims to analyse the shifting balance of power between the ruler and the merchant class in Dubai. For this purpose, it relies on an historical institutionalist approach, which divides historical development into periods of 'path dependency' and 'critical junctures.' The second article in the trilogy, "The Dubai Model," published in 2009 analyses the economic logic behind the current developmental drive and explore and outline the Dubai model of economic development. The final article in the trilogy from 2011, titled "Economic and Institutional Reforms in the Arab Gulf Countries" basically asks the question, to which extent the Dubai model serves as a model for other Gulf countries and thus focuses on the degree to which the model can be replicated.

The motivation to write this – the first – article derives from three observations. First, from a neo-liberal globalist point of view, the state-centric development model applied in Dubai prompted the question, what role the private sector has or should play in such societies. Second, the dominating discourse in explaining the observed development in Dubai in the late 1990s was to focus on the person and actions of its ruler Muhammad bin Rashid. In other words, the developmental achievements were reduced to an a-historic action by a single man. To provide a more nuanced understanding of the apparent development, the paper sets out to explore the origins and institutionalization of the much-acclaimed pro-business environment in Dubai. A third and related observation was that the literature largely missed to link Dubai's developmental achievements with its government structures.

The theoretical point of departure in this paper is developmental state theory and in particular the neo-statist writer Peter Evan's notion of 'embedded autonomy.' The concept of the developmental state is "shorthand for the seamless web of political, bureaucratic, and moneyed influences that structures economic life in capitalist Northeast Asia" (Woo-Cumings 1999, 1). Evans claims that the most successful states developmentally possess two unique features, i.e. a well-functioning bureaucracy, and dense ties between the public and the private sector. To Evans the public-private ties perform essential functions related to the developmental effort of the state.

This paper argues that Dubai has the basic characteristics of a developmental state and sets out to explore one of its features, i.e. the public-private ties as they unfold in the authoritarian and neo-patrimonial setting of Dubai.

Three research questions are analysed: 1) what has been and what role is the private sector to play in Dubai's development strategy? 2) how has the ruler-merchant power balance evolved over time, and 3) which formal and informal channels exist through which the public and private sector currently interact?

The role of the private sector in Dubai's developmental trajectory is defined by the strategic move it made in the early 19th century, where Dubai succeeded in attracting an international trading and business community from the pearl trading city of Lingar in Persia. The promises given to the merchants to persuade them to relocate to Dubai established the pro-business environment and came to constitute a critical juncture and institutionalised a new development path in which pro-activity and a pro-business environment rose to key prominence. The development strategy was to expand the economy by emphasizing growth in the private sector by attracting merchants from the region to set up business in Dubai.

In reference to the second question, I found that the power balance between the ruler and the merchants changed considerably over time due to fluctuations in the economic standing of the two parties. From a situation of mutual dependence and strength, it changed during the pre-oil era where the merchants' proceeds from the pearling business plummeted and the ruler's financial position sharply improved due to 'rents' from the British. The ruler's economic strength made way for a cooptation of the merchant class into a neo-patrimonial state structure where the merchant class received financial patrimonial-clientelistic favours in exchange for their complete political compliance. In the 1980s and onward, Dubai pursued a development strategy that sought to maximise the benefits of globalization for example through attracting Foreign Direct Investments (FDI). Hence, the ruler–merchant power balance had turned in favour of the merchants (now the internationalised business community).

The third working question is concerned with the specific public-private ties in present-day Dubai. The article argued that there exists an interplay between the various public and private actors and that this interplay is characterised by a lack of formal institutions, structures, or channels that link the two sectors. However, the article argues that several informal channels exist. Notably, the *majlis*, the 'open-door' policy and not least 'leadership through multiple roles.'

Thus, the analyses show how the sheikhs, the merchants, and parts of the wider business community are linked through various and dense public–private ties. Ties that distinctively blur the distinction between the public and the private sector, but act as two-way streets. On one hand, ties that allow the ruler (or government) to stay well informed about business matters and secure a rapid and consistent implementation of its visions. On the other hand, ties that allow the internationalised business community present in Dubai to voice their concerns to the ruler and to place pressure on him to accommodate its wishes.

This article represents my first attempt to understand the developmental trajectory of Dubai. The institutional focus implied in the historical institutionalist perspective revealed that the foundation of Dubai's current developmental trajectory was the deliberate effort by the Maktoum ruler around 1900 to attract a merchant class from Persia and not – as commonly perceived – to the advent of oil or the accent of the current ruler Sheikh Muhammad bin Rashid al Maktoum to power in the early 1990s. That effort constitutes the critical juncture that placed Dubai on an institutional path of a pro-business environment and continued emphasis on attracting capable business people.

This paper contributes to Gulf studies in several ways. First, as a novelty this article introduced developmental state theory into the studies of the Arab Gulf states and analysed one aspect of embedded autonomy, i.e. the density of the public-private ties. Developmental state theory in the context of the Arab Gulf states is further developed and applied in the second article in the trilogy, i.e. the 'Dubai Model' article, and will be discussed in the subsequent summary. Second, while literature on patrimonialism, state legitimacy, and more generally states in the Arab Gulf countries (Ayubi 1995; Davidson 2005; Hudson 1977; Niblock and Malik 2007; Owen 2004) has discussed the cooptation of the private sector into the public sector and the resulting 'blurredness' of distinctions between the two sectors, this study contributes with a detailed and specific analysis of the nature and degree of the interconnectedness between the two sectors. Thirdly, why historical writings on Dubai (e.g. Davidson 2005; Heard-Bey 2004) have dealt with the issue of attracting the new merchant class from Persia to Dubai, I believe that my study if not the first then among the first to interpret this event in an institutional perspective and thus view it as the foundation of an institutionalization of the pro-business environment in Dubai.[63] Fourth, I believe that this paper contributes with an expansion of our understanding of the link between state structures and development in the Gulf region.

---

63 See Young (2014), who seven years later published an historical institutionalist analysis of the political development in UAE.

Publication 3

Hvidt, Martin. 2009. "The Dubai Model: An Outline of Key Development-Process Elements in Dubai." *International Journal of Middle East Studies*. 41 (3): p. 397-418.

This article, the second of the trilogy, is motivated by an academic quest to understand, explain, and analyse both the content and the process of the noteworthy development that had unfolded in Dubai from the early 1990s. The article explores the hypothesis that a special 'Dubai model' of economic development can be identified.

At the time of publishing, the developmental process of Dubai had hardly been analysed by academics. In this perspective, the article is innovative. Four questions are addressed in this publication: 1) what characterises the state in Dubai, 2) what have been the key parameters of its development path since 1990, 3) what are the economics of the undertaking, and 4) whether or not the chosen path is sustainable?

At the outset, the article is seeking to understand the nature of the state in Dubai, which on the one hand can be characterised as authoritarian, rent-based, neo-patrimonial, and highly tribal,[64] and on the other, is extremely pro-market and neo-liberalistic. A review of 'state models' served to identify cross-state and cross-regional varieties of such models. On behalf of this exercise, it is found that the developmental model applied in Dubai closely resembles the model pursued in the East Asian development states. The so-called developmental state theory was brought into the analysis and revealed several basic features that influence the depth of state interventions in these economies. As summed up by White and Wade (1988, 24), these interventions encompass a "historical legacy of strong and economically active states, traditions of social and political hierarchy and strong nationalist sentiments underpinned by cultural homogeneity and reinforced by external threats."

Situating Dubai among – or at least as being significantly inspired by – the Asian developmental models – especially that of Singapore – provided a platform for understanding the developmental trajectory of Dubai from a developmental state theoretical perspective. The importance of documenting the link between the developmental model in East-Asia and

---

64 Tribalism and kinship structures are underplayed in this publication but figure more prominently in later publications, see especially Publication 9.

the developmental model in Dubai, lies in the possibility to depart from particularistic interpretations to universalistic ones in studying Dubai's developmental undertakings.

According to the second research question that relates to the specific parameters of the developmental drive, the article identifies nine such parameters: Government-led development (ruler-led), fast decision-making and "fast track" development, flexible labour force, bypass of industrialization—creation of a service economy, internationalization of service provision, creation of investment opportunities, supply-generated demand ("first mover"), market positioning via branding, and development in cooperation with international partners.

According to the third research question, i.e. concerning the economics of the Dubai development path, the article explores the highly puzzling question of how Dubai generates the financial means to sustain and not least develop its society, taking into account the very modest revenues from oil, few taxes levied on individuals and businesses, and the extensive financial incentives provided to foreign companies in the economic free zones? The article finds that service-related fees and fees from public utilities, oil, state-owned enterprises, lease of government-owned housing, and sale of land and property, forms the primary sources of income.[65] The article points out that it is likely that the sales of land to foreign investors has made up the largest economic contribution (turning 'sand into gold,' so to speak). While it is likely that land sales in the future will contribute less, it is pointed out that the income that originates in hosting international firms and a large cohort of expats will likely increase. In this way, state ownership of service providers like telephone companies, electricity, water, air carriers and an ability to levy fees on day-to-day necessities, e.g., drivers licenses, domestic workers, etc. all make it economically logical to keep ownership of service providers on state hands, and not least to expand population size through immigration.

The final issues discussed in the article relate to the sustainability of the 'Dubai Model.' A number of vulnerabilities are listed, originating in both internal and external factors and both of an economic, political, and environmental nature.

The paper contributes to the scholarly field of Gulf studies in important ways: First, through an account of the specific parameters of the Du-

---

65 In retrospect, the financial crisis commencing in 2008 revealed that Dubai had also built a portfolio of public loans worth 130 billion dollars to finance the developmental drive. The loan issue is underplayed in this text, since the extent of government lending was not known prior to the crisis.

bai model, this paper testifies that the developmental trajectory followed in Dubai lends itself to multi-causal explanations. Second, while the state plays an enormously important role in the developmental drive in all of the allocation states in the Gulf, this paper suggests a new theoretical approach to interpret the state in Dubai, and possibly in other Gulf countries, i.e. developmental state theory. Third, the paper represents the first scholarly attempt to explain and analyse the logic of the economics behind the developmental drive and academically coins the term the 'Dubai model.' Fourth, the term 'model' however does not imply that all parts of the model can be replicated by other states in the region. The specific context in which the model has evolved is the likely reason for that. In a review, the article was said to offer "a ground-breaking analysis of the development process in Dubai." [66]

Publication 4

Hvidt, Martin. 2011. "Economic and Institutional Reforms in the Arab Gulf Countries." *Middle East Journal.* 65 (1): p. 85-102.

This article is the third in the trilogy that set out to explore the unique developmental trajectory of Dubai. The hypothesis to be tested in this article is the extent to which the 'Dubai model' is replicated in the surrounding Gulf countries.

While it was – and is – evident that the other Gulf countries replicate the overt features of the model, such as the built environment,[67] 'world class' facilities to cater to the international businesses,[68] and a strategic focus on selected international high-growth sectors – notably aviation and tourism – this article explores and analyses to what extent the surrounding Gulf states replicate the production-oriented features of the Dubai model, i.e. implementing reforms related to the business environment,

---

66 By the assessment committee which reviewed me qualified for the rank as full professor in 2011. The committee consisted of Professor Dietrich Jung, Center for Contemporary Middle East Studies, University of Southern Denmark, Professor Mervat Hatem, Howard University, Department of Political Science, Washington DC, and Professor Jørgen Bæk Simonsen, Institute for Cross-cultural Studies, Copenhagen University.
67 For example, skylines in glass, luxury living spaces located on artificial islands and not least extravagant malls.
68 For example, free zones and attractive office space and light taxation regimes.

infrastructure, economic diversification, inflation, and improvements in the educational system.

More specifically, using Luciani's (1987) distinction between 'allocation states' and 'production states', the article examines to what degree the Gulf countries are changing or adjusting their underlying economic structure (i.e. through economic reforms), making way for a more production-oriented economic structure. The article assumes that, since economic reforms are both time-consuming and politically difficult to implement, such reforms are only implemented if a government has compelling reasons to do so. That is, either if a government are forced to do it maybe as a result of an economic crisis, or if the decision-makers have an explicit aim to restructure the economy, thus transforming the present-day allocation state model into a more production-oriented one.

The article conducts three analyses to determine whether the Gulf states are reforming to adopt a production-oriented economic model, 1) it establishes whether or not the six Gulf states can in fact be said to be allocation states, 2) an analysis of the degree to which the Gulf countries have implemented economic reforms and the content of these reforms, and 3) an analysis of the inflow of FDI conducted to establish how the international business community has responded to the reforms made.

The first analysis firmly places the six Gulf states as allocation states since between 62% and 80% of state income derives from the sales of hydrocarbons in all states. While this might not come as a surprise for a Gulf researcher, the data to prove this point are only rarely presented.

The second analysis traces the status of the competitiveness of the economies and the reforms implemented over the past decade. The data source for this analysis and interpretation are two indexes, i.e. the *Doing Business Index* by the World Bank and the *Global Competitiveness Index* published by the World Economic Forum.

The first thing noted, is that the Gulf countries obtain the best rankings within the group of MENA countries on the Doing Business Index indicating that they as a group represent the most business-friendly environments in the region. Worldwide, Saudi Arabia and Bahrain ranked among the 25 most business-friendly. Saudi Arabia and UAE improved their ranks over the time period investigated, while Kuwait and Oman had fallen to lower ranks. Qatar and Bahrain are placed high on the index, but had not been rated before, which does not lend itself to conclusions.

The Competitiveness Index bases its ranking on assessments on 12 so-called pillars, such as; institutions, infrastructure, macroeconomic environment, health and primary education, market efficiency, labour market efficiency, technological readiness, etc. All six Gulf countries are placed among the 40 most competitive economies in the world in 2010-2011, and the competitiveness of all but one of the six countries have improved over the last 5 years, allegedly due to reforms related to the business environment, infrastructure, economic diversification, inflation, and improvements in the educational system.

It is noted that there is a considerable variation among the six countries, and among their scores on each of the pillars. All the Gulf economies do well according to 'basic requirements,' while performing less well on 'efficiency enhancers' (among them education, labour market efficiency), and even lower on 'innovation and sophistication' factors. Hence, this index places the Gulf economies as factor-driven or efficiency-driven. Only UAE has reached a level of sophistication that leads to a classification as an innovation-driven economy. One conclusion drawn from the data and the analysis is that significant reforms are needed in three areas: education, investment in R&D, and in the organization and regulation of the labour markets.

The third analysis presented data on the inflow of FDI and used these as a proxy for the success of the economic reforms assuming, maybe a bit simplistic, that the more reform toward a market-friendly way, the more FDI will be attracted. The data shows a significant increase in the inflow of FDI from 2000 to 2007. However, for 2008 and 2009 the economic crisis affected the reported figures. It is argued that two major reasons lie behind this increase, reforms in the regulatory environment of foreign investments to meet international standards, and probably of more importance, opening up larger parts of the Gulf economies to foreign investments, e.g., in property, and in the oil and gas sector.

Based on these analyses, the article concluded that the six Gulf countries had in fact been implementing economic and institutional reforms during the decade after the year 2000 that were instrumental in laying the groundwork for production-oriented economies. Furthermore, the paper concluded that while this is certainly an important initial step for the states in reaching their stated aims of diversifying their economies and revitalizing the role of the private sector, rolling back 30 to 50 years of rentierism is not a process that can be done easily or hastily.

The contribution of the article to Gulf studies is as follows. First, while it had been customary in the rentier state theory literature both implicitly and explicitly to call for both economic and political reforms in the Gulf countries to place the economies on a more solid foundation, such calls are rarely made specific. This article explicates the type of reforms to be pursued and the sectors they should target to change from an allocation economy to a production-oriented economi. Hence, the article firmly places economic reforms as vehicles of transformation on the agenda in Gulf studies. Furthermore, the article is an expression of a universalistic research approach to the region. Second, the article introduces the data behind the *Doing Business Index* and the *Global Competitiveness Index* into the scholarly field of Gulf studies. While business magazines and newspapers over the years had picked key indicators from these indexes and reported them, this article is the first academic study that uses the data embedded in the indexes to analyse ongoing reform processes in the Gulf countries. One likely reason for this might have been that Bahrain and Qatar were not included in the indexes until 2009.

Publication 5

Hvidt, Martin. 2012. "Planning for Development in the Arab Gulf States: A content Analysis of Current Development Plans." *Journal of Arabian Studies*. 2 (2): p. 189-207.

In Publication 4 above, I had assumed that the decision-makers in the Gulf had a long-term aim to depart from the allocation state model and to introduce a production-oriented and neo-liberal economic model. However, evidence from the field brought this assumption into question. Hence, this article shifts the focus of my studies from the past and current developmental trajectory to the future developmental trajectory of the six Gulf countries. Through a content analysis of the most recent development plans published in the region, this study aimed to provide insight into how leaders and decision-makers in the Gulf countries understand or perceive the challenges facing their economies and how they propose to meet them.

Furthermore, the paper analyses aspects of state planning as it unfolds in the context of the Arab Gulf countries and focuses on the type of planning, i.e. rational-comprehensive vs. new-style planning, the ideational underpinning of the planning effort, and the capacity of the states to actually implement the plans.

Five questions guided the content analysis carried out in this article, i.e. 1) what barriers to growth are envisioned in the plans and how can they be anticipated, 2) what economic sectors and activities will be stimulated to create jobs and future income streams, 3) will the public or the private sector be the driver of the future economy? 4) what type of (economic) state is envisioned in the future? and 5) what is the ideational input underpinning the planning effort?

The following conclusions were drawn from this study: First, the plans express dissatisfaction with the current economic model, i.e. the 'allocation-state' model. This model is seen as causing a host of problems, among them, unsustainability, volatility, lack of job creation and income formation, and a significant import of labour. Diversification of the economy away from dependence on oil and gas incomes is highlighted to overcome these problems.

Second, the plans aim to build 'created comparative advantages,' implying that current oil revenues should be invested in economic activities and assets that will enable the country to compete internationally and generate future income streams. First and foremost, investments should be allocated to the high growth sectors in the globalised economy for example aviation, tourism/hospitality, real estate, logistics, business services, manufacturing, and 'high-technology-content products' like smart or green technologies.

Third, most of the countries envisage a continuation of the state-led developmental model, but with a positive mention of a future role for the private sector. Hence, the reviewed development plans do not embrace the dominating neo-liberal doctrine. The state remains the driver of the economy through its substantial development budget and ownership of firms, while the private sector is confined to operate in niches where the state has chosen not to invest, e.g., in trading, retail, or construction. However, Bahrain and Oman aim to create a neoliberal, free market economy, where the private sector (as opposed to the state) is the driver of the economy and where meritocracy is to be (re-)introduced into the public sector through real competition.

Fourth, the plans envisage a gradual shift from the allocation-state model to a more production-oriented model, where the state, the citizens, and the private sector are encouraged to be involved in producing actual goods and services, and where the government increasingly relies on proceeds from this production to finance the society.

Fifth, the analysis of the ideational underpinning of the planning found that the aims and efforts were perceived to be within the globally dominant discourse of neoliberal economics passed on by the international consultancy firms. In addition, from interviews with planners and decision makers in the region, the paper identifies two meta-ideas, closely related to development and planning, i.e. the application of a 'cluster' approach and a 'world-class city' approach. Both these approaches are found to provide a blueprint for fast, centralised action to be taken by the government and both envisaged development as being initiated in a 'big push' fashion, with multiple initiatives being pursued simultaneously to get development up and going. The world-class city approach underpinned the general conception that cities, not individual industries or states, compete on the international scene for jobs and investments.

The last part of the paper is a discussion of the degree to which development planning indeed expresses the future growth trajectory of the region. Deficiencies in the state administrative systems are found to be resulting from the state-building efforts undertaken under the impact of abundant incomes from oil and expressed in Hertog's notion of 'segmented clientelism.' These administrative weaknesses make it difficult to anticipate successful implementation of the broader reform initiatives called for in the development plans.

Despite this, it is concluded that the development plans and the planning process represent more than just 'window dressing.' In each Gulf country, interview data pointed to serious intentions of reform among parts of the decision-making elite. In this respect, formulation of plans must be seen as the first step in articulating a reform agenda. Hence, development plans and visions are a part of an important political process of clarifying the policy aims that must take place in each of the Gulf states.

This paper contributes to the academic field of Gulf studies in several ways. First, it introduces development planning, the discipline and the tools, into the academic field of Gulf studies.[69] Second, as a novelty within Gulf studies, this article uses development plans as a primary source of data as background for a systematic understanding of how the decision-makers in the region perceive the future for their countries and, not least, what challenges they are facing to achieve their planning goals. To use plans as an academic source, though, has its challenges. Third, this article explicated the complex link between the goals of planning, the specific Gulf context, and the vehicles used for implementation, i.e. the 'cluster' approach and the 'world-class city' approach.

---

69 This does not imply that no researcher had touched upon the subject before, e.g., Rodney Wilson, a renowned scholar of the Middle East, published a short research paper in 1983 in which he researched the impact of foreign influences in development planning in Egypt, Syria, and Saudi Arabia (Wilson 1983). See also Mallakh (1966); Ghanem (2001).

Publication 6

Hvidt, Martin. 2013. *Economic Diversification in the GCC Countries – Past Record and Future Trends.* **LSE Research Paper series no. 27: Kuwait Programme on Development, Governance and Globalisation in the Gulf States. London: The London School of Economics and Political Science (LSE). 51 pp.**

This paper is written in conjunction with the previous article. They both address questions related to the future development path of the Gulf states, and although they both use developmental plans as their primary source of data (however, in this paper only for one out of several analyses), they differ significantly in focus. Publication 5 focuses on the planning process, its goals, and the capabilities of the states to carry out planning, while this paper conducts an in-depth analysis of one long-standing and overriding developmental goal, i.e. economic diversification. Despite overlaps between the two publications (pp. 34-38 in this paper closely resemble pp. 195-198 in Publication 5), the different analytical focus it applies and the considerably longer format of this paper vs. the article, merit that both publications are included in this dissertation.

This study was commissioned by the 'Kuwait Programme on Development, Governance and Globalisation in the Gulf States' at the London School of Economics. The author was invited to submit a proposal for a study on economic diversification, which found its final form through a peer-review process. When submitted, the full paper went through yet another peer review process before publication. The paper is widely read both by academics and practitioners and has been downloaded in excess of 3900 times from the LSE website since publication.[70]

The paper analyses and discusses the concept of economic diversification and strategies to implement it. As is evident from planning documents, official announcements, and policy initiatives economic diversification is a key concept for understanding the development drive in the Gulf states. The obvious reason for this emphasis relates to the three sets of risks associated with the near total reliance on hydrocarbons as income earners, i.e. that the resources are finite, the income from gas and

---

70 By 10 December 2018, see http://eprints.lse.ac.uk/cgi/stats/report/eprint/55252

oil fluctuates over the year and across years, and lastly, that oil and gas incomes tend to crowd out other income sources.

The aim of the study is to provide a comparative assessment of the diversification effort in each of the Gulf countries, through an analysis of how the developmental plans relate to each other (similarities and differences) and how they contribute to broader prospects for diversification in each country. Furthermore, the paper aims to identify structural and political barriers to further diversification.

In the literature on the Arab Gulf, in developmental plans, and in actual decision-making the concept of diversification is rarely defined and is often used in an all-encompassing sense and not least, as a cure to all economic ills. This paper contributes to an understanding of the concept by differentiating between horizontal and vertical diversification and applies the concept of diversification to a Gulf context, i.e. in relation to industrialization, oil sector development, private sector, and sovereign wealth funds. Furthermore, the paper discusses and specifies how to measure the concept.

I found that, in a Gulf context, diversification takes on a broader meaning than just risk reduction. It represents what could be considered an attempt to return to economic 'normality', i.e. a production-oriented society. The sudden influx of oil wealth that commenced in the 1950s and 1960s disrupted the previous long term developmental trajectory based on trade, pearling (until the 1930s), and various types of subsistence production. Oil income brought sudden wealth, which offered possibilities for rapid development of the countries, including infrastructure build-up, provision of 'cradle-to-coffin' welfare states, and comfortable lifestyle. However, it also crowded out the traditional income sources and dis-encouraged the emergence of substantial new productive activities (especially in the small Gulf states, i.e. not Saudi Arabia) and in this way established itself as the sole income source. However, as argued throughout my writings, the resulting developmental model can no longer be sustained facing high demographic growth rates and fluctuating oil prices. Hence, the 'oil-plenty-era' should rightfully be seen as an 'anomaly' in the long-term developmental trajectory of the region.

This paper finds that decision-makers in the Gulf states use the term of diversification broadly as re-implementing economic 'normality', which means to return to a production-oriented mode of operation in the economies, where there are multiple income sources, where the private sector plays a more pronounced role in wealth and job creation, where the process of hiring and firing is based on merits, and generally, where income both for society and for each individual depends on the yields from the productive activities.

Furthermore, the paper finds that over the last five decades, the Gulf states have taken various important steps en route to diversifying their economies away from dependence on oil and gas. First, education and health systems have been created. Second, infrastructure essential for economic activity and diversification, e.g., roads, harbours, telecommunication, has been built. Third, a variety of manufacturing industries, primarily servicing an international market, have been established.

Commencing in the early 2000s, important economic reforms have been undertaken in some of the countries (though not in Qatar and Kuwait), aiming to attract investments, both from nationals and foreigners, to their economies.

Despite these efforts, data show that the countries remain in a situation where their economies are highly dependent on the oil sector and that few of the industries and services established would survive in a post-oil era. So, the Gulf states continue to be in a situation where they sell only one commodity, i.e. their hydrocarbons on the world market, and use the proceeds to import almost all their living requirements and not least, large parts of their labour force. Viewed in this perspective, so far, the diversification drive has largely failed.

Structural barriers to diversification are found in the bleak forecasts of World Wide growth, negatively affecting the prospects for start-up companies in manufacturing and service activities (this has become even more pronounced after the paper was published with the 2014 oil price collaps), and in the significant duplication of economic activities within the Gulf region not only in energy-intensive areas such as petrochemicals, steel and aluminium, but also in tourism facilities, aviation, real estate, banking and education. Furthermore, diversification is found to be impeded by a significant lack of interregional trade and cross-border infrastructures, which dampen the possibilities of reaping the benefits of a more integrated and enlarged economic space. It is also impacted by a broader lack of interregional corporation and trust, resulting in low levels of coordination, e.g. of the establishment of important cross-border infrastructural projects (most notably the Gulf railway project) and of economic policies (this has become even worse since June 2017 where the so-called 'Qatar crisis' has led to further rifts among the Gulf states).

Political barriers to diversification is found to lie in the so-called 'ruling bargain' or 'social contract' that exists between the rulers and the citizens in the Gulf societies. If pursued seriously, the diversification drive (i.e., the specific reforms aimed at facilitating diversification) as devised and printed in the development plans, will essentially take away time-honoured privileges from the local population in an attempt to redress the link between effort and reward and to slowly transfer job creation for nationals to the private sector.

The political response to the Arab Spring in 2011 was analysed to measure the robustness of the political pursuit of the reform initiatives. A simple question was asked, i.e. faced with a crisis, will the decision-makers adhere to the reform agenda they themselves have embarked on? The paper finds that, in a time of crisis, ad hoc measures take precedence over plans. Furthermore, the Gulf governments were not only ready to abandon their long-heralded policies of diversification, they were even willing to implement measures that directly contradicted them. However, this paper recognises that the situation concerning the Arab Spring might not be the most suitable litmus test of political commitment to the diversification process due to the perceived severity of the situation, i.e. that it could be life-threatening to the regime. (A more appropriate case for this analysis would be to study the policy initiatives taken to curb governmental spending following the near halving of the yearly oil incomes starting in 2014).

The contribution of this paper to the scholarly field of Gulf studies encompasses, first, a clarification and definition of the concept of diversification in a Gulf context, second, an updated review of the diversification programmes and policies undertaken so far in the region, based on field study, interviews in each of the six Gulf countries, and an analysis of the development plans, and third, in the identification of structural and political barriers which the current diversification drive is facing.

Publication 7

Hvidt, Martin. 2015. "The State and the Knowledge Economy in the Gulf: Structural and Motivational Challenges." *The Muslim World*. 105 (1): p. 24-45

This article represents an attempt to specify and analyse another of the key developmental concepts pursued and applied by decision-makers in the Arab Gulf countries, i.e. the concept of 'knowledge economy.' Like the concept 'diversification,' this concept is rarely appropriately defined when used in development plans, policy statements, or even in the limited number of academic publications addressing the subject in the Arab Gulf. Hence, the application of the concept is diffuse, lacks analytical precision, and often appears as a generic term for the type of 'developed society' which the Gulf countries are aiming to become.

This paper seeks to make a contribution to the current literature and policy debates by defining and discussing the concept of knowledge economy, and to apply it to an Arab Gulf context. Furthermore, the paper discusses the motivation or incentives which the young Gulf Arabs have to pursue a role within the knowledge economy.

The paper is the outcome of an invitation to participate in the 'Working group on State and Innovation in the Gulf' hosted by the Center for International and Regional Studies (CIRS), Georgetown University, Qatar during 2013 and 2014. The paper was subsequently published in the journal *The Muslim World* as part of a special issue on 'Innovation and the Knowledge Economy in the Arab Gulf countries.'

The article analyses the challenges faced by the Gulf states to successfully transform their distributional economies into knowledge economies. It pursues this aim through analyses of the reasons why the Gulf states exhibit dismal performance on two of the four pillars that the World Bank applies to define a knowledge economy, i.e. education and innovation.

At the outset, the paper argues that a transformation to a knowledge economy is neither just about the number of citizens who hold a higher education degree, nor is it primarily an endeavour with an emphasis on natural science-based innovations, but as pointed out by Stiglitz (1999, 6-8), it is more broadly about societies possessing a culture which focuses on citizens' participation, ownership of processes, and active learning so that motivation, aspirations, and entrepreneurship becomes intrinsic ethos of the individual.

The general approach to promote the transition to knowledge economies followed by planners and politicians in the region focuses on expanding education, increase in research funding, providing science parks, and establishing incubators for young entrepreneurs,[71] all of which are without doubt important and purposeful undertakings. However, this article addresses what the author considers to be a more fundamental issue

---

71   These elements of the transition to knowledge economies were the key items discussed in the conference "Setting the Stage for A Knowledge-based economy in the Gulf – With a focus on Qatar," organized by HEC Paris in Qatar, Qatar National Research Fund and Qatar University, Doha, Qatar 25th -27th October 2016.

in the creation of knowledge economies in the Gulf countries, i.e. the incentives, or lack hereof, which the young Gulf Arabs face when choosing to pursue academic studies or engage actively in a knowledge economy. This paper discusses incentives under the headings of structural and motivational factors.

As documented through an analysis of the World Bank's *Knowledge Economy Index* the Gulf states have not only fallen behind in international comparison on the two pillars of education and innovation, they are also underperforming in these areas in relation to their sizeable GDPs.

The article pursues analyses of the quality of the primary, secondary, and tertiary educational systems. The overall finding is that current educational systems by and large do not prepare the students adequately for either pursuing further studies or engaging actively in a knowledge economy. To act comfortably in such an economy, the students should have undergone an educational system that would have taught them skills related to critical thinking, analysis, active learning, ownership of processes, and innovative drive. In addition, the national school systems characterised by root learning, lack of curriculum reforms and teachers with inadequate training, provide little inspiration and thus motivation to pursue academic studies. Furthermore, the social and economic realities are found to provide few incentives for the young Gulf Arabs to pursue deep professional knowledge or to become active and engaged knowledge workers.

For several generations, the basic structure of the economy, i.e. the distributional state, have secured jobs and income and more generally, a well-off and comfortable lifestyle for the national population. However, as hypothesised in rentier state theory, a 'rentier mentality' has emerged among nationals where 'rewards' are disconnected from 'work.' The article analyses the incentive structures and argues that the Gulf societies offer very few incentives for the young generations to work hard, become risk taking entrepreneurs, pursue long and difficult university degrees, or apply a long-term perspective to climbing a career ladder.

Furthermore, it is argued that the short time elapsed since schooling was introduced at a broader scale in the Gulf states, and the fast-changing demands in relation to relevant knowledge, present significant challenges related to the transfer of knowledge from the past to the current generation. Finally, it is argued that the massive size of the expat labour force and the lack of professional career paths for nationals also negatively impacts the incentives. Hence, it is concluded that economic and social realities provide little incentive for young Gulf Arabs to pursue deep professional knowledge or to become active and engaged knowledge workers.

The contribution of this article to Gulf studies lies within two areas, first by reviewing the definition of knowledge economies and applying the concept to an Arab Gulf context. Second, by putting the sensitive and tacit issue of motivation of the young Gulf Arabs on the research agenda of Gulf studies. As is evident from the reference list of the paper, only very few studies have been conducted focusing on this issue. This is in sharp contrast to the role that human capital more generally is set to play in the broader developmental processes.

Publication 8

Hvidt, Martin. 2018. "The United Arab Emirates: Modernity and Traditionalism in Petroleum Sector Management." In *Public Brainpower: Civil Society and Natural Resource Management*, edited by Indra Overland, 311-328. Cham: Palgrave Macmillan.

This book chapter combines two aspects of the UAE society, which I have not explicitly dealt with earlier, i.e. UAE decision-making structures and the energy sector.

The chapter is a contribution to a major research project nested at the Energy Programme at the Norwegian Institute of International Affairs (NUPI) aiming at analysing the interlinkages between the socio-political system and the management of the petroleum sector in different countries. While most of the Resource Course literature analyses how natural resources and revenues affect society, this research project flips the question and asks how society influences the way that the petroleum sector is managed. The central thesis of the NUPI project is that successful long-term management of the petroleum sector depends on factors like freedom of speech, a dynamic and wide-ranging public debate, and an active civil society that engages in petroleum sector issues.

This chapter explores the nature of decision-making in the UAE to analyse the public debate and the role of various actors in influencing how oil and gas resources and revenues are managed in the UAE.

As mentioned above in discussing data scarcity, none of the Gulf countries are, nor strive to be, 'democracies' in the sense of a liberal Western multi-party system. The UAE maintains a decision-making structure based on a traditional tribal system, characterised by centralised decision-making, personalised rule, and consensus among the group of decision-makers, counterbalanced with the practice of consultation with the elders and tribal heads within society. Phrased in social science terms, the type of governance is autocratic and neo-patrimonial and thus, does not encourage transparency in decision-making, public debates, e.g., in news media, let alone criticising decisions taken.

This chapter argues that the governance structure tends to dampen the public debate in all domains, especially those that relate to domestic issues. This, in combination with factors like a high level of trust in the traditional system of rule by the population, and not least ambiguous laws relating to libel and slander that create unclear boundaries for what can safely be uttered in public, leaves little space for public debate. Furthermore, as argued in the book chapter, this translates into an absence of organised interest groups within society.

The chapter analyses the case of the implementation of nuclear power in the UAE to highlight the lack of public debate. Nuclear power is not only a sizeable energy investment but arguably a decision that could be expected to give rise to considerable public debate in the news media. The analysis found that at least in the written news media in the UAE, there is no genuine public debate on critical energy issues.

The second main issue addressed in the chapter relates to the institutions governing the energy sector and notably, the decision-making structures and processes in the UAE. The chapter argues that the current decision-making structure in the UAE and more specifically in Abu Dhabi represents a continuation of the traditional tribal system of rule. While the road to modern statehood for most countries possessing tribal structures has included deliberate attempts to curb the strength of the tribes to shift loyalty from the tribal groups to the state, this has been less apparent in the UAE. For example, Van Der Meulen (1997, 8) points out that "political leadership [in the UAE] is confirming, legitimizing, strengthening, and extending the role of tribal and kinship ties in politics and the management of the economy." The consequence is that the traditional structure of rule in Abu Dhabi allows decisions concerning the development of the petroleum sector, and its incomes, to be made by a small group of people belonging to the ruling family and their associated elites. The composition of the Supreme Petroleum Council in Abu Dhabi underscores this point. In line with the tribal and dynastic nature of the royal families in the Gulf countries, the majority of the members in this council are members of the royal family in Abu Dhabi, the rest from long serving elite families.

Thus, the paper finds that the persisting tribal elements in the decision-making structure are prominent and not least have tangible consequences for day-to-day decision-making. For example, it allows one of the seven emirates making up the United Arab Emirates, Abu Dhabi, to govern app. 85% of the UAE oil wealth.

Hence, the article establishes that the royal family is the key decision-maker within the energy sector. Furthermore, it argues that it is plausible that the sector is managed both in a qualified and professional manner with the aim to optimise export earnings and satisfying the need for local energy consumption.

A final question raised and analysed in this chapter is how the members of the royal family keep informed and not least up-to-date with the rapidly changing advancement in technology and economic opportunities that characterises the oil business.

It is argued that the deliberate decision to keep international oil companies involved in the hydrocarbon sector and the international approach pursued in the development of nuclear power underscores the understanding that the country's decision-makers rely heavily on international consultants and companies to provide ideas, operational experience and expertise, and probably also strategic guidance in the development and future planning of the sector.

Hence, petroleum sector management in UAE negates the overall hypothesis of the NUPI research project, that successful long-term management of the petroleum sector depends on factors like freedom of speech, a dynamic and wide-ranging public debate and an active civil society that engages in petroleum sector issues. What the UAE case shows is that sizeable revenues from oil can translate into a significant import of outside expertise, either international consultants or companies to manage their energy sector. Abu Dhabi seems to pursue a pragmatic middle course where they can involve international expertise to ensure a successful long-term management of the petroleum sector and at the same time maintain their authoritarian and neo-patrimonial state structure.

The contribution of this article to the scholarly field of Gulf studies lies, first in a more nuanced understanding of the structure and logic of the political system in UAE. Hence, this paper contributes to the relatively limited body of academic publications that analyse how traditional tribal/kinship-based structures translate into, and replicate themselves, in the current political system.[72] Second, this paper contributes academic

---

72 A renewed recognition of the role that tribes are playing in state affairs and culturally

insight into the political economy of energy as it plays out in an oil-rich Gulf state.

Publication 9

Hvidt, Martin. Forthcoming. "Highly-skilled Migrants and their Contribution to Development: Exploring the nexus between the *Kafala* system, highly skilled migrants and societal growth in United Arab Emirates. *Journal of Arabian Studies*.[73]

This study explores the nexus between economic growth in the Arab Gulf states and immigration of highly-skilled migrants. While an abundance of academic studies related to the role, motivations and not least working conditions of low-skilled workers in the Gulf region exists, studies analysing issues related to highly-skilled migrants are indeed very rare. Furthermore, while it is generally assumed that highly skilled migrants contribute significantly to growth and development, few studies have explicated this relationship especially in a Gulf context. Hence, this article aims to contribute to this significantly understudied topic.

This paper, as the 'Knowledge Economy' article summarised above (Publication 7), is an outcome of an invitation from the Center for International and Regional Studies (CIRS), Georgetown University, Qatar to participate in a Working group. It was titled *Highly Skilled Migrants: The Gulf in Comparative Perspective* and ran during 2016 and 2017.

The migrant labour force is of paramount importance for the Gulf economies. Approximately, half of the population in this region today consists of migrants and in countries like Qatar and the UAE, which are used as case studies in this paper, their share of the population is close to 90%. Approximately one quarter of these are classified as highly-skilled migrants.

The aim of the article is to explore the nexus between economic growth in the Arab Gulf states and immigration of highly-skilled migrants. Hence, the article reviews contemporary economic growth models and

---

are visible e.g., in Cooke (2014) and in the newly initiated research programme at London School of Economics titled: 'Qabila in the 21st Century. The Role of Tribes in the Domestic Politics of the Gulf' (see http://www.lse.ac.uk/middle-east-centre/research/kuwait-programme/projects/tribes).

73 See footnote 3.

asks which role highly-skilled migrants play in the growth processes? It is deduced that only technological progress will lead to long-term growth in economies, and the paper analyses to which degree highly skilled migrants in fact contribute to technological progress.

The analyses are conducted within the overall policies of the so-called *Kafala* system which is the broader framework through which migrant flows to the Gulf countries have been managed since the mid-1970s. Four research questions guide the analyses: 1) Do the skills of the highly-skilled migrants complement or overlap the skills of nationals? 2) How are migrants selected to enter the Gulf countries? 3) What incentives and disincentives does the *Kafala* system offer the highly-skilled to fully contribute to the economy? and 4) To what extent is knowledge transfer between migrants and nationals being pursued?

It was argued that the skills of the migrants complement rather than overlap with the skills of the local population. Furthermore, the *Kafala* system represents a stringent version of a demand-oriented migrant selection system, which is instrumental in ensuring labour market success, understood as a speedy entry into the job market after arrival and employment throughout the duration of the stay in the country.

However, the analysis of incentives found that the asymmetric power balance between sponsor and migrant, the built-in inflexibility in relation to job mobility, with the resulting tendency to keep overqualified migrants employed, and not least the lack of a broader sense of inclusion through more permanent forms of residency, provide reduced incentives for the highly-skilled migrants to fully embrace the UAE economy and thus, to contribute to their long-term economic growth. A culture of transience was found to prevail, which results in short-term thinking, implying less innovation, less emphasis on long-term capability building, and less likelihood of entrepreneurship.

In addition, and more specifically related to technological progress, it was found that technology transfer, aside from the transfer that takes place within the educational system, most likely bypasses the local population due to demographic realities (very few nationals compared to expats) and the general educational level in society. When and if technology transfer takes place, it most likely takes place between two migrants.

It is beyond doubt that highly-skilled immigrants have contributed significantly to elevating the UAE to theirs current developmental stage by filling gaps in the human resources in society. However, as this paper points out, while the current framework to attract and retain highly-skilled migrants assures an efficient selection process and high labour market success, issues related to a prevalent culture of transience and a low degree of technology transfer prevails, and consequently negatively impacts the potential benefit of this workforce for the country. Thus, the overall conclusion of this study is that the UAE society does not take full advantage of their stock of highly-skilled migrants and thus, forgo developmental opportunities.

This study contributes to the field of Gulf studies in two ways: First, it provides insight into a significantly understudied studied topic, i.e. that of highly-skilled migrants in the Gulf. Second, as pointed out by one of the anonymous reviewers of the paper, the "argument concerning technological progress and its role in fostering development is a welcome addition in our understanding of economic development and highly skilled migration in the Gulf."

4 Conclusion

Above, the nine publications included in this dissertation have been summarised individually and their respective and detailed contribution(s) to the scholarly field of Gulf studies have been accounted for.

This dissertation has – I believe – made several theoretical contributions to Gulf studies. First, the introduction of 'developmental state theory' as an alternative theoretical perspective to the hegemonic rentier state theory. As pointed out, developmental state theory is statist by nature. It emphasises effective statecraft and focus on what Evans (1995, 6) calls the 'transformative role' of states i.e. the capacity of the state to facilitate entrepreneurship and the creation of new productive capacities. Thus, the theory advocates a dynamic and proactive role of the state, and claims that growth and wealth creation should no longer be seen just as a function of nature and markets, but can be created, given appropriate state interventions. In other words, this theoretical perspective lets us analyse and understand state structures and roles, relations between state and society, and not least, how states contribute to development.

Developmental state theory, which was developed to analyse and explain the performance of the high growing Asian economies in the second part of the 20th century, has proven highly applicable for the studies carried out in this dissertation, both as an analytical and explanatory tool. The centralised decision-making structure found in the Arab Gulf countries, the 'late-late-late' entry into development, the urge to 'catch up' with the West, and not least, the funds to pursue 'created comparative advantages' all resonate with this theoretical perspective.

In this dissertation, developmental state theory has been applied as a statist perspective and, more specifically, as an analytical tool related to the embedded nature of the state, i.e. the links or 'ties' between key actors in Arab Gulf societies, notably the public and private sector. Equally important, it has been applied, both directly and indirectly, in analyses that focus on state capacity and efficiency of their bureaucracies.

However, the application of developmental state theory has not reached its full analytical potential as a theoretical basis for analyzing the Arab Gulf states. This is due to the lack of both insight into – and data related to – the inner workings of the bureaucracies.

Developmental state theory provides an alternative theoretical perspective in the study of the highly centralised, statist, and kinship-based states in the Gulf region than offered by rentier state theory. This will likely lead to other and alternative explanations to the observed growth than the rentier state theories could or did, when data become available.

A second area in which this dissertation has made a theoretical contribution to the scholarly field of Gulf studies is by its explicit critique of rentier state theory. It has done so by ascribing agency to the decision-makers and planners. In classical rentier state theory, decision-makers within rentier states are envisioned to act as passive distributors of the (unlimited) oil wealth. In this dissertation, detailed empirical studies have shown that this is not the case. On the contrary, throughout my studies, it has been documented, how states and the decision-makers have attempted, some even very eagerly, to place their countries on a developmental trajectory that aimed at diversification of the economies and a return to a 'production-based' mode of operation to place their economies on a more solid production-oriented footing.[74]

The critique levied toward rentier state theory in this dissertation stems from three sources. First, as mentioned, the empirical studies, which have documented actual development undertakings and planned initiatives. Second, through the planning-related focus applied throughout the dissertation. Planning, whether physical, economic, or social represents a willful desire to implement changes to a given society and to translate these desires into actual implementation – in other words, planning fundamentally presumes agency. Hence, emphasizing planning

---

74   As mentioned, my studies related to Dubai, were used by Gray (2011) to suggest a 'third phase' rentier state model. See section 2.4.1.2.

in the studies of the Gulf negates the basic premise of rentier state theory. Third, through the application of a developmental state theoretical perspective, which, as argued above, assumes statism, i.e. state-centric actions, targeted to overcome developmental barriers.

A third theoretical contribution to the scholarly field of Gulf studies by this dissertation is the application of an explicit institutional focus, notably historical institutionalism. As an analytical tool, institutions have been viewed as permanent features of historical development and have encouraged studying the dynamic interplay between periods of critical junctures and those of path dependency in the developmental trajectory of the Gulf. The Gulf context has undergone manifest changes and thus critical junctures over the past century, such as the discontinuation of the pearling industry, the advent of incomes from oil, and the resulting radical change of society, e.g., migration, institutionalization of the *Kafala* system, etc. Hence, applying an institutional focus has facilitated both a long-term and historically informed perspective on development and an improved understanding of the possibilities for – and barriers against – change, both at the societal and the individual level.

Empirically, the dissertation has been successful in documenting and analyzing the 'Dubai Model of economic development', which provided a hitherto undocumented reference point for discussions of developmental trajectories, not only in Dubai but more generally, in the smaller Gulf states. Furthermore, the studies have been the first to explicitly address the issue of planning, and to introduce development plans as useful and legitimate textual sources to an improved understanding of the developmental goals pursued by the decision-makers in the Gulf states. In addition, the studies have introduced the various indexes, e.g., the *Doing Business Index* and the *Global Competitiveness Index* into the scholarly field of Gulf studies. Finally, my research has placed the Gulf countries in the developmental sequence as 'Late-late-late' developers, thus placing attention on both the possibilities and the constraints this late entry into the developmental process has for the developmental choices and thus, the trajectories they can pursue.

In recognizing that development lends itself to multifaceted explanations, I have found it academically fruitful to base this dissertation on a variety of topics (and theories), which represent a selection of what (Stern 1989, 669) designates the 'Grand issues' within the academic discipline of development economy: State structures, institutions, developmental paradigms, and planning; income earning activities, e.g., natural resources, industrialization, services; demographic growth and human capital building; labour market issues and migration; international trade, globalization, balance of payment issues and investments.

Each of the enclosed studies is to be considered a 'brick' in a larger structure that constitutes the pool of qualified theoretical and empirical knowledge related to the developmental trajectory of the modern Arab Gulf states.

On the methodological level, the dissertation represents a normalization of the analysis of the Gulf states, in that it refrains from treating the developmental trajectory of the Arab Gulf states as being 'exotic' or exceptional outside the mainstream humanistic and social sciences. This dissertation has applied a universalistic approach, in which general theories (mainly originating within development economics) and methodological tools have been applied, thus allowing comparative analysis both among the six Gulf states, and maybe even globally.

However, even from a universalistic perspective, this group of countries displays a set of characteristics that make them significantly different from other countries under development; i.e. their late entry into the development process (as 'late-late-late' developers), the abundance of capital they have at their disposal to underpin their developmental process, and lastly, excluding Saudi Arabia, the diminutive size of the native population. These features have created a context for development, which is significantly different from the context found in most developing countries, and especially among the capital poor and labour abundant countries not only in Africa or Asia but within the Middle East and the North African region itself (e.g., Egypt, Iran, Iraq, Morocco).

Cammett et al. (2015, 23ff) argue that a nexus exists between resource endowments and political development within the states in the Middle East and North African region. This dissertation hypothesises that a nexus between resource endowment and economic development exists for the Gulf countries.

While several resource-rich countries, e.g., Iraq, Iran, Libya, Syria, and, outside the region, especially Nigeria and Venezuela, have had difficulties in translating high oil incomes into development for their citizens, which appears not to be the case in the Arab Gulf states. At the overarching level, this dissertation has found reason to hypothesise that such a nexus exists in the Arab Gulf states, not only due to the size of the incomes pr. capita, but plausibly due to the encompassing and distributive features nested within the tribal, kinship and rentier based governance systems.

There is plenty of evidence that oil wealth has been squandered, particularly in the earlier years of the oil boom (1970s), that oil incomes have continued to underpin a highly uneven income distribution, and not least, have been instrumental in delaying necessary reforms. However, the ruling elites in the Gulf have deliberately channelled massive funding not only into improving the living standard of society at large, but also into a broader developmental process, which over the last 50 years has been among the fastest in the world.[75] Statistics related to the parameters at the HDI index, i.e. Life Expectancy at Birth, Infant Mortality and Years of Schooling all testify to massive developmental advances since the early 1970s.[76]

While this dissertation recognises and applauds this positive development, the research and analyses carried out through the individual studies encompassed in this dissertation have primarily focused on the detrimental and disrupting effects related to the economic 'anomaly' created by the sudden and massive influx of oil revenues, such as the growth of rentier mentality, the crowding out of productive activities, and the lack of economic diversification. However, while the Arab Gulf countries have attempted to diversify their economies away from oil in order to create jobs for the national population and make their economies less vulnerable to oil price fluctuations, their dependency on the incomes from oil has in fact continued to increase. As such, the key challenge remains namely how and not least when, the Arab Gulf countries will make a societal change to pursue a development trajectory, which is both economically and socially sustainable.

I believe that the present volume and the nine publications encompassed in this dissertation viewed in its entirety contribute to the advancement of science in the scholarly field of Gulf studies, by theoretical and empirical-based analyses of the development trajectory pursued in the modern Gulf States. Broad-reaching and nuanced empirical work, has been seen as foundational for an improved understanding of the developmental path and trajectory of the region. While the scholarly field of Gulf studies has advanced significantly during the last decade, there is still much to be achieved before a more comprehensive and theory-based understanding of this trajectory can be reached.

---

75 See e.g. El Katiri, Fattouh, and Paul (2012, 183) that conclude that Kuwait successfully has used its oil income to improve the living standard of its people and that these benefits have reached all citizens.
76 See for example Cammett et al. (2015, 162 and 4) or UNDP (2016, Table 2: Trends in the Human Development Index, 1990-2015)

References

Aghion, Philippe, and Peter Howitt. 2009. *The Economics of Growth*. Cambridge, Massachusetts: MIT Press.

Al-Fahim, Mohammed. [1995] 2007. *From Rag to Riches: A story of Abu Dhabi*. Abu Dhabi: Makarem G. Trading and Real Estate (LLC).

Al-Kuwari, Al-Khalifa. 1978. *Oil Revenues in the Gulf Emirates: Patterns of Allocation and Impact on Economic Development*. Boulder: Westview.

Al-Muslimi, Farea. "A History of Missed Opportunities: Yemen and the GCC." Carnegie Middle East Center, Accessed 23 March 2017. http://carnegie-mec.org/diwan/62405.

Amenta, Edwin. 2012. "Historical Institutionalism." In *Political Sociology*, edited by Edwin Amenta, Kate Nash and Alan Scott, 47-56. Chichester, West Sussex: Wiley-Blackwell.

Amin, Samir. 1974. *Accumulation on a World Scale*. 2 vols. New York: Monthly Review Press.

Anderson, Ewan W. 2000. *The Middle East: Geography & Geopolitics*. London: Routledge.

Auty, Richard M. 2001. "Introduction and Overview." In *Resource Abundance and Economic Development*, edited by Richard M Auty, 3-16. Oxford and New York: Oxford University Press.

Ayubi, Nazih N. 1995. *Over-stating the Arab State: Politics and Society in the Middle East*. London: I. B. Tauris.

Babbie, Earl. 2013. *The Practice of Social Research* 13th Edition. International Edition ed. Canada: Wadsworth Gengage Learning.

Baldwin-Edwards, Martin (Ed.) 2011. *Labour immigration and labour markets in the GCC countries: national patterns and trends, Research Paper No. 15: Kuwait Programme on Development, Governance and Globalisation in the Gulf States*. London: London School of Economics and Political Science (LSE)

Basedau, Matthias, and Patrick Köllner. 2006. *Area Studies and Comparative Area Studies: Opportunities and Challenges for the German Institute of Global and Area Studies (GIGA), A discussion Paper*. Hamburg: German Institute of Global and Area Studies (GIGA).

Beblawi, Hazem. 1987. "The Rentier State in the Arab World." In *The Rentier State*, edited by Hazem Beblawi and Giacomo Luciani, 49-62. London: Croom Helm.

Beblawi, Hazem, and Giacomo Luciani (Eds.). 1987. *The Rentier State*. London: Croom Helm.

Beck, Martin. 2007. "Der Rentierstaats-Ansatz und das Problem abweichender Fälle." *Zeitschrift für Internationale Beziehungen* 14 (1): 43-69.

Binder, Leonard. 1976. "Area Studies: A Critical Reassessment." In *The Study of the Middle East: Research and Scholarship in the Humanities and the Social Sciences*, edited by Leonard Binder, 1-28. New York: John Wiley & Sons.

Cammett, Melani, Ishac Diwan, Alan Richards, and John Waterbury. 2015. *A Political Economy of The Middle East*. Boulder, Colorado: Westview Press.

Cavazza, Stefano. 2017. "Suspicious Brothers: Reflections on Political History and Social Sciences." *Ricerche di Storia Politica* 30 (Special Issue on Political History Today: Power, Subjects, Categories): 53-64.

Chatelus, Michel. 1990. "Policies for Development: Attitudes toward Industry and Services." In *The Arab State*, edited by Giacomo Luciani, 99-128. Berkeley, Los Angeles: University of California Press.

Cooke, Miriam. 2014. *Tribal Modern: Branding New Nations in the Arab Gulf*. Berkeley: University of California Press.

Crystal, Jill. 1990. *Oil and politics in the Gulf: Rulers and Merchants in Kuwait and Qatar*. Cambridge: Cambridge University Press.

Davidson, Christopher M. 2005. *The United Arab Emirates: A Study in Survival*. Boulder: Lynne Reinner.

———. 2006. "After Shaikh Zayed: The Politics of Succession in Abu Dhabi and the UAE." *Middle East Policy* 13 (1): 42-59.

———. 2009. *Abu Dhabi: Oil and Beyond*. London: Hurst & Company.

———. 2012. *After the Sheikhs: The coming collapse of the Gulf Monarchies*. London: Hurst & Company.

Davis, Mike. 2006. "Fear and Money in Dubai." *New Left Review* 41 (October 2006): 47-68.

El Katiri, Laura, Bassam Fattouh, and Segal Paul. 2012. "Anatomy of an oil-based welfare state: Rent distribution in Kuwait." In *The Transformation of the Gulf. Politics, Economics and the Global Order*, edited by David Held and Kristian Ulrichsen, 165 - 87. London: Routledge.

Evans, Peter B. 1989. "Predatory, Developmental and Other Apparatuses: A comparative Political Economy Perspective on the Third World State." *Sociological Forum* 4 (4): 561-87.

———. 1995. *Embedded Autonomy: States and Industrial Transformation*. New Jersey: Princeton University Press.

———. 2005. "The Challenges of the 'Institutional Turn': Interdisciplinary Opportunities in Development Theory." In *The Economic Sociol-*

ogy of Capitalist Institutions, edited by Victor Nee and Richard Swedberg, 90-116. Princeton, NJ: Princeton University Press.

Evans, Peter B., Dietrich Rueschemeyer, and Theda Skocpol. 1985. *Bringing the State Back In*. Cambridge: Cambridge University Press.

Field, Michael. 1985. *The Merchants: The Big Business Families of Saudi Arabia and the Gulf States*. Woodstock, New York: The Overlook Press.

Foley, Sean. 2010. *The Arab Gulf States: Beyond Oil and Islam*. Boulder, Colorado: Lynne Rienner.

Fox, John W., Nada Mourtada-Sabbah, and Mohammed al-Mutawa. 2006a. "The Arab Gulf region: Traditionalism globalized or globalization traditionalized?" In *Globalization and the Gulf*, edited by John W. Fox, Nada Mourtada-Sabbah and Mohammed al-Mutawa, 3-59. London: Routledge.

―――. 2006b. *Globalization and the Gulf*. London: Routledge.

Frank, Andre Gunder. 1966. "The Development of Underdevelopment." *Monthly Review* 18 (4): 17-31.

Freer, Courtney. 2017. "Rentier Islamism in the Absence of Elections: The political role of Muslim Brotherhood affiliates in Qatar and the United Arab Emirates." *International Journal of Middle East Studies* 49 (3): 479-500.

Gardner, Andrew M. 2011. "Lazy Arabs: A Reconceptualization of the Qatari "Rentier Economy"." *Paper presented at Society for Applied Anthropology annual meeting*. Seattle, Washington, March 31, 2011.

―――. 2012. "Why Do They Keep Coming? Labour Migrants in the Persian Gulf States." In *Migrant Labour in the Persian Gulf*, edited by Mehran Kamrava and Babar Zahra, 41-58. London: Hurst & Co.

Gause, Gregory F. 1994. *Oil Monarchies: Domestic and security challenges in the Arab Gulf States*. New York: Council on Foreign Relations.

―――. 1990. *Saudi-Yemeni relations*. New York: Columbia University Press.

―――. 2010. *The International Relations of the Persian Gulf*. Cambridge: Cambridge University Press.

Gerschenkron, Alexander. [1962] 1966. *Economic Backwardness in Historical Perspective. A Book of Essays*. Cambridge, Massachusetts: The Belknap Press of Harvard University Press.

Ghanem, Shihab M. 2001. "Industrialization in the UAE." In *United Arab Emirates. A new perspective*, edited by Ibrahim Al-Abed and Peter Hellyer, 260-76. London: Trident Press.

Gore, Charles. 2000. "The Rise and Fall of the Washington consensus as a Paradigm for Developing Countries." *World Development* 28 (5): 789-804.

Gray, Matthew. 2011. *A Theory of 'Late Rentierism' in the Arab States of the Gulf, Occasional Paper No. 7*. Doha: Center for International and Regional Studies, Georgetown University School of Foreign Service in Qatar.

Gylfason, Thorvaldur 2001. *Natural Resources and Economic Growth: From Dependence to Diversification*. Paper prepared for an Expert Group Meeting on Economic Diversification in the Arab World organized by The United Nations Economic and Social Commission for Western Asia (UN-ESCWA) in cooperation with the Arab Planning Institute (API) of Kuwait, held in Beirut, Lebanon, 25-27 September, 2001.

Hall, Peter A., and Rosemary C. R. Taylor. 1996. "Political Science and the Three new Institutionalisms." *Political Studies* XLIV: 936-57.

Hanieh, Adam. 2011. *Capitalism and Class in the Gulf Arab States*. New York: Palgrave Macmillan.

Heard-Bey, Frauke. 2001. "The Tribal Society of the UAE and its Traditional Economy." In *United Arab Emirates. A new perspective*, edited by Ibrahim Al-Abed and Peter Hellyer, 98-116. London: Trident Press.

———. 2004. *From Trucial States to United Arab Emirates*. Dubai: Motivate Publishing.

Hendrix, Gullen S, and Marcus Noland. 2014. *Confronting the curse: The Economics and Geopolitics of Natural Resource Governance*. Washington DC: Peterson Institute for International Economics.

Henry, Clement M., and Robert Springborg. 2001. *Globalization and the Politics of Economic Development in the Middle East*. Cambridge: Cambridge University Press.

Henry, Clement Moore, and Robert Springborg. 2010. *Globalization and the Politics of Development in the Middle East*. Second Edition. Cambridge: Cambridge University Press.

Herb, Michael. 1999. *All in the Family. Absolutism, Revolution, and Democracy in the Middle Eastern Monarchies*. New York: SUNY.

———. 2017. *Ontology and methodology in the study of the resource curse, LSE Kuwait Programme Paper Series no. 43*. London: London School of Economics and Political Science (LSE)

Hertog, Steffen. 2010. *Princes, Brokers, and Bureaucrats: Oil and the State in Saudi Arabia*. Ithaca: Cornell University Press.

———. 2014. "Redesigning the Distributional Bargain in the GCC." In *Gulf Politics and Economics in a Changing World*, edited by Michael

Hudson and Mimi Kirk, 29-54. Singapore: World Scientific.

Hertog, Steffen, and Giacomo Luciani. 2013. *Workshop preamble: The Rentier State at 25: Dismissed, Revised, Upheld?* Fourth Gulf Research Meeting (GRM), Cambridge, 1 - 5 July 2013, organized by the Gulf Research Center Cambridge (GRCC) at the University of Cambridge.

Hirschman, Albert O. [1958] 1969. *The Strategy of Economic Development*. New Haven: Yale University Press.

Hudson, Michael C. 1977. *Arab Politics: The Search for Legitimacy*. New Haven: Yale University Press.

Hvidt, Martin. 1996. "Løgn, forbandet løgn, og statistik. Om brugen af statistisk materiale om og fra Mellemøsten." *Tidskrift för mellanösternstudier (TfMS)* 1996 (1): 85-96.

Issawi, Charles. 1970. "Middle East Economic Development, 1815-1914: The General and the Specific." In *Studies in the Economic History of the Middle East from the rise of Islam to the present day*, edited by M. A. Cook, 395-411. London: Oxford University Press.

———. 1982. *An Economic History of the Middle East and North Africa*. London: Methuen & Co.

———. 2004. "Middle East Economic Development, 1815-1914: The General and the Specific." In *The Modern Middle East: A Reader*, edited by Albert Hourani, Philip Khoury and Mary C. Wilson, 177-93. London: I. B. Tauris.

Jones, Larry E., and Rodolfo E. Manuelli. 2005. "Neoclassical Models of Endogenous Growth: The effects of Fiscal policy, Innovation and Fluctuations." In *Handbook of Economic Growth*, edited by Philippe Aghion and Steven N. Durlauf. Amsterdam, The Netherlands: Elsevier B.V.

Jung, Dietrich. 2016. "Centre for Contemporary Middle East Studies: A Multi-Disciplinary Approach." *Tidsskrift for Islamforskning* 10 (1): 36-53.

Kamrava, Mehran, and Zahra Babar (Eds.). 2012. *Migrant Labour in the Persian Gulf*: Hurst & Co.

Kanna, Ahmed. 2007. "Dubai in a Jagged World." *Middle East Report* 243: web version, no pagination. http://www.merip.org/mer/mer243/dubai-jagged-world.

Khalidi, Rashid I. 2003. "The Middle East as an Area in an Era of Globalization." In *Localizing Knowledge in a Globalizing World: Recasting the Area Studies Debate*, edited by Ali Mirsepassi, Amrita Basu and Frederick Weaver, 171-90. Syracuse, N.Y.: Syracuse University Press.

Khalifa, Ali Mohammed. 1979. *The United Arab Emirates: Unity in Fragmentation*. Boulder Colorado: Westview Press.

Kostiner, Joseph (Ed.) 2000. *Middle East Monarchies: The Challenge of Modernity*. New York: Lynne Rienner.

Kropf, Annika. 2016. *Oil Export Economies: New comparative perspectives on the Arab Gulf States*. Berlin: Gerlach Press.

Kubursi, Atif A. 1999. "Prospects for Regional Economic Integration After Oslo." In *Middle East Dilemma. The Politics and Economics of Arab Integration*, edited by Michael C. Hudson, 299-319. London: I. B. Tauris.

Kubursi, Atif A. 1984. *Oil, Industrialization & Development in the Arab Gulf States*. London: Croom Helm.

Kuznets, Simon. 1967. *Modern Economic Growth: Rate Structure, and Spread*. New Haven and London: Yale University Press.

———. 1973. "Modern Economic Growth: Findings and Reflections." *The American Economic Review* 63 (3): 247-58.

Lacey, Robert. 2009. *Inside the Kingdom: Kings, Clerics, Modernists, Terrorists and the Struggle for Saudi Arabia*. New York: Arrow Books.

Lewis, W. Arthur. 1984. "The State of Development Theory." *The American Economic Review* 74 (1): 1-10.

Lockman, Zachary. 2010. *Contending Visions of the Middle East: The History and Politics of Orientalism*. Second Edition. New York: Cambridge University Press.

Lorimer, J. G. [1915] 2003. *Gazetteer of the Persian Gulf, Oman and Central Arabia*. 6 vols. London: Archive Editions.

Lucas, Robert E. 1988. "On the Mechanics of Economic Development." *Journal of Monetary Economics* 22: 3-42.

Luciani, Giacomo. 1987. "Allocation vs. Production States: A Theoretical Framework." In *The Rentier State*, edited by Hazem Beblawi and Giacomo Luciani, 63-82. London: Croom Helm.

———. 2005. "Oil and Political Economy in the International Relations of the Middle East." In *International Relations of the Middle East*, edited by Louise Fawcett, 79-104. Oxford: Oxford University Press.

———. 2012. "Introduction: Resources Blessed: Diversification and the Gulf Development Model." In *Resources Blessed: Diversification and the Gulf Development Model*, edited by Giacomo Luciani. Germany: Gerlach Press.

Ludden, David. 2003. "Why Area Studies?" In *Localizing Knowledge in a Globalizing World: Recasting the Area Studies Debate*, edited by Ali Mirsepassi, Amrita Basu and Frederick Weaver, 131-6. Syracuse, N.Y.: Syracuse University Press.

Mahdavy, Hussein. 1970. "The Patterns and Problems of Economic Development in Rentier States: The Case of Iran." In *Studies in Economic History of the Middle East*, edited by M. A. Cook, 428-67. London: Oxford University Press.

Mallakh, Ragaei El. 1966. "Planning in a Capital Surplus Economy: Kuwait." *Land Economics* 42 (4): 425-40.

Martinussen, John Degnbol. 2005. *Society, State & Market: A Guide to Competing Theories of Development*. London: Zed Books.

Meier, Gerald M., and James E. Rauch. 2005. *Leading Issues in Economic Development*. Eighth Edition. New York: Oxford University Press.

Ménoret, Pascal. 2005. *The Saudi Enigma*. London: Zed Books.

———. 2014. *Joyriding in Riyadh: Oil, Urbanism, and Road Revolt*. Cambridge: Cambridge University Press.

MESA. 2017. *MESA Program for the 51st Annual Meeting (preliminary version 9. sep. 2017)*. Washington D.C.: MESA.

Mirsepassi, Ali, Amrita Basu, and Frederick Weaver. 2003. "Introduction: Knowledge, Power, and Culture." In *Localizing Knowledge in a Globalizing World: Recasting the Area Studies Debate*, edited by Ali Mirsepassi, Amrita Basu and Frederick Weaver, 1-21. Syracuse, N.Y.: Syracuse University Press.

Mitchell, Timothy. 2004. "The Middle East in the Past and Future of Social Science." In *The Politics of Knowledge: Area Studies and the Disciplines*, edited by David L. Szanton, 74-118. Berkeley: University of California Press.

Mørch, Søren. 1996. "Mellemøststudier ved Odense Universitet." *Mellemøstinformation* (1): 16-9.

Niblock, Tim (Ed.) 1980. *Social and economic development in the Arab Gulf*. London: Croom Helm.

Niblock, Tim, and Monica Malik. 2007. *The Political Economy of Saudi Arabia*. London: Routledge.

Nielsen, Helle Lykke. 1997. ""Den grimme ælling – erfaringer fra et praksisorienteret forsknings- og formidlingscenter." In *Imod en ny videnskabelig dannelse: Sider af universitetets undervisning og kultur*, edited by Anne-Marie Mai, Jørgen Gleerup, Peter Dahler-Larsen and Bent Ørsted, 49-68. Odense: Odense Universitetsforlag.

———. 2006. "Praksisorienterede mellemøststudier ved Syddansk Universitet." In *Eventyrere og orientalister: Studier over dansk orientalistiks historie tilegnet Svend Søndergaard på 75-årsdagen den 5. maj 2006*, edited by Johan Hermann Rump, 31-45. København: Forlaget Vandkunsten.

North, Douglass C. 1990. *Institutions, Institutional Change and Economic*

Performance. New York: Cambridge University Press.

———. 1991. "Institutions." *Journal of Economic Perspectives* 5 (1): 97-112.

Owen, Roger. 2004. *State, Power and Politics in the Making of the Modern Middle East*. London: Routledge.

Peters, Guy B., Jon Pierre, and Desmond S. King. 2005. "The Politics of Path Dependency: Political Conflict in Historical Institutionalism." *The Journal of Politics* 67 (4): 1275-300.

Polany, Karl. [1944] 2001. *The Great Transformation: The Political and Economic Origins of Our Time*. Boston: Beacon Press.

Porter, Michael E. 1998. "Clusters and the New Economics of Competition." *Harvard Business Review* (November-December 1998): 77–90.

Ramakrishnan, A. K., and M. H. Ilias (Eds.). 2011. *Society and Change in the Contemporary Gulf*. New Delhi: New Century Publications.

Robinson, Jeffery. 1988. *Yamani: The Inside Story*. London: Simon Schuster.

Rodrik, Dani, and Mark R. Rosenzweig. 2009a. "Development Policy and Development Economics: An Introduction." In *Handbook of Development Economics, Volume 5*, edited by Dani Rodrik and Mark R. Rosenzweig, 4039-5061. Amsterdam, The Netherlands: Elsevier B.V.

——— (Eds.). 2009b. *Handbook of Development Economics, Volume 5*. Edited by Kenneth J. Arrow and Michael D. Intriligator. Amsterdam, The Netherlands: Elsevier B.V.

Romer, Paul M. 1986. "Increasing Returns and Long-Run Growth." *Journal of Political Economy* 94 (5): 1002-37.

Rosenstein-Rodan, Paul N. 1943. "Problems of Industrialisation of Eastern and South-Eastern Europe." *The Economic Journal* 53 (210/211): 202-11.

Rostow, Walt Whitman. 1960. *The stages of growth: an non-Communist manifesto*. Cambridge: Cambridge University Press.

Rump, Johan Hermann (Ed.) 2006. *Eventyrere og orientalister: Studier over dansk orientalistiks historie tilegnet Svend Søndergaard på 75-årsdagen den 5. maj 2006*. København: Vandkunsten.

Samin, Nadav. 2017. "Interpreting the Oil Kingdom: Opportunities and Hazards." *International Journal of Middle East Studies* 49 (3): 526-8.

Schumpeter, Joseph A. 1961. *The Theory of Economic Development: An Inquiry into Profits, Capital, Credit, Interest, and the Business Cycle*. New York: Oxford University Press.

Schäbler, Birgit. 2007. *Area Studies und die Welt: Weltregionen und neue Globalgeschichte*. Wien: Mandelbaum Verlag.

Sick, Gary. 2009. "The United States and the Persian Gulf in the Twentieth Century." In *The Persian Gulf in History*, edited by Lawrence G.

Potter, 295-310. New York: Palgrave Macmillan.

Stern, Nicholas. 1989. "The Economics of Development: A Survey." *The Economic Journal* 99 (397): 597-685.

Stiglitz, Joseph E. 1999. *Public Policy of a Knowledge Economy*. London: Department for Trade and Industry and Center for Economic Policy Research.

———. 2002. *Globalization and its discontents*. London: Penguin Books.

Szanton, David L. 2004. "The Origin, Nature, and Challenges of Area Studies in the United States." In *The Politics of Knowledge: Area Studies and the Disciplines*, edited by David L. Szanton, 1-33. Berkeley: University of California Press.

Tessler, Mark, Jodi Nachtwey, and Anne Banda. 1999. "Introduction: the Area Studies Controversy." In *Area Studies and Social Science: Strategies for Understanding Middle East Politics*, edited by Mark Tessler, Jodi Nachtwey and Anne Banda, vii-xxi. Bloomington: Indiana University Press.

Tétreault, Mary Ann, Andrzej Kapiszewski, and Gwenn Okruhlik. 2011. "Twenty-First-Century Politics in the Arab Gulf States." In *Political Change in the Arab Gulf States: Stuck in Transition*, edited by Mary Ann Tétreault, Gwenn Okruhlik and Andrzej Kapiszewski, 1-18. Boulder and London: Lynne Rienner.

Thirlwall, A. P. 2006. *Growth & Development: With Special Reference to Developing Economies*. Eighth Edition. Houndsmills, Basingstoke: Palgrave Macmillan.

Todaro, Michael P., and Stephen C. Smith. 2011. *Economic Development*. Eleventh Harlow, England: Pearson/Addison-Wesley.

———. 2015. *Economic Devleopment*. Twelfth Edition. Harlow, England: Pearson.

Ulrichsen, Kristian Coates. 2016a. "Economic Diversification Plans: Challenges and Prospects for Gulf Policymakers." In *The AGSIW Visions of Change Series*. Washington: The Arab Gulf States Institute in Washington.

———. 2016b. *The Gulf States in International Political Economy*. Houndsmills, Basingstoke, Hampshire: Palgrave Macmillan.

———. 2017. *The United Arab Emirates: Power, Politics, and Policymaking*. London: Routledge.

Ulrichsen, Kristian Coates (ed.). 2012. *The Political Economy of Arab Gulf States*. Cheltenham, UK: Edward Elgar Publishing.

UNDP. 2016. *Human Development Report 2016: Human Development for*

Everyone, New York. United Nations Development Programme.

Valbjørn, Morten. 2008. *A 'Baedeker' to IR's Cultural Journey Before, During and After the Cultural Turn – Explorations into the (Ir)relevance of Cultural Diversity, the IR/Area Studies Nexus and Politics in an (Un)exceptional Middle East.* Århus: Forlaget Politica.

———. 2009. "Exploring the IR/Area Studies Nexus - tracking pathways 'downwards' in different cultural-institutional contexts." In *Papers presented at the annual meeting of the International Studies Association, New York City, US.* New York.

Valbjørn, Morten, and Lars Erslev Andersen. 2005. "Mellemøsten: En (u)almindelig region." In *Mellemøsthåndbogen: Fakta om Landene i Mellemøsten og Nordafrika*, edited by Lars Erslev Andersen, Søren Hove and Maj Vingum Jensen, 115-30. Odense, Denmark: Syddansk Universitetsforlag.

Valeri, Marc. 2009. *Oman. Politics and Society in the Qaboos State.* London: Hurst & Company.

Van Der Meulen, Hendrik. 1997. *The Role of Tribal and Kinship Ties in the Politics of the United Arab Emirates.* The Fletcher School of Law and Diplomacy: University microfilms international.

Waldner, David. 1999. *State Building and Late Development.* Ithaca: Cornell University Press.

Weil, David N. 2009. *Economic Growth.* Boston: Pearson/Addison Wesley.

———. 2016. *Economic Growth.* (Third Edition) London and New York: Routledge.

White, Gordon, and Robert Wade. 1988. "Developmental States and Markets in East Asia: An Introduction." In *Development States in East Asia*, edited by Gordon White, 1-29. Houndsmills: Macmillan Press.

Williamson, John. 2003. "From Reform Agenda to Damaged Brand Name. A short history of the Washington Consensus and suggestions for what to do next." *Finance and Development* 40 (3): 10-3.

Wilson, Rodney. 1983. *Development Planning in the Middle East: The Impact of Foreign Influences.* Conflict Studies. Research Paper Number 156. London: The Institute for the Study of Conflict.

———. 1987. *Gulf trade and finance: Trends and market prospects.* London: Graham and Trotman.

Wolfensohn, James D. 1998. *The Santiago Consensus - From Vision to Reality.* Presidential speech, World Bank President, Santiago, April 19, 1998.

Woo-Cumings, Meredith. 1999. "Introduction: Chalmers Johnson and the Politics of Nationalism and Development." In *The Developmen-*

tal State, edited by Meredith Woo-Cumings, 1-31. Ithaca and London: Cornell University Press.

Yalcin, Serhat. 2018. "Book review: The political economy of energy, finance and security in the United Arab Emirates. Between the Majilis and the market by Karen E. Young." *British Journal of Middle Eastern Studies* 45 (1): 119-20.

Yergin, Daniel. 1991. *The Prize: the Epic Quest for Oil, Money & Power*. New York: Touchstone, Simon & Schuster.

———. 2011. *The Quest: Energy, Security, and the Remaking of the Modern World*. London: Allen Lane/Penguin Group.

Young, Karen E. 2014. *The Political Economy of Energy, Finance and Security in the United Arab Emirates: Between the Majilis and the Market*. Houndmills, Basingstoke: Palgrave Macmillan.

Zahlan, Rosemarie Said. 1978. *The Origins of the United Arab Emirates: A Political and Social History of the Trucial States*. Houndsmills: The MacMillan Press.

Aarts, Paul, and Gerd Nonneman (Eds.). 2006. *Saudi Arabian in the Balance: Political Economy, Society, Foreign Affairs*. London: Hurst & Company.

5. Summary in Danish / Dansk resumé

Denne afhandling er udarbejdet som en antologi, som omfatter denne publikation samt ni andre. De inkluderede artikler, bogkapitler og et research-paper repræsenterer et udvalg af de publikationer, der er resultatet af forskning, jeg har gennemført siden 2003, da jeg første gang rettede min akademiske opmærksomhed mod den unikke og højst bemærkelsesværdige udvikling, som kan observeres i de arabiske golfstater.

Udviklingen i de arabiske golfstater er gået hurtigt. For eksempel har hovedstaden i De Forenede Arabiske Emirater, Abu Dhabi, i løbet af blot 60 år udviklet sig fra en fattig fiskerby med under 10.000 indbyggere, selvsagt uden skoler eller hospitaler eller andre faciliteter, til en moderne og rig by med over 2,5 millioner indbyggere, en Hong-Kong-lignende skyline og alle tænkelige faciliteter.

Set i et udviklingsperspektiv må Golflandene betragtes som 'outliers', da disse har haft rigeligt med penge til at finansiere deres udviklingsproces til forskel fra fattigere lande i Afrika, Asien og Latinamerika. Som påpeget i nærværende afhandling kan penge løse en række udviklingsmæssige problemer, men langt fra alle.

Overordnet undersøger jeg med denne afhandling, hvordan beslutningstagere i de arabiske golfstater, det vil sige Bahrain, Kuwait, Oman, Qatar, Saudi Arabien og UAE (De Forenede Arabiske Emirater) begrebsliggør og gennemfører udvikling i samfund hvor: befolkningen blot to generationer tilbage stort set ikke havde modtaget uddannelse. Hvor industrialiseringen er i sin vorden, statsindtægterne primært stammer fra én kilde, nemlig eksport af olie og gas, og hvor den moderne stat og det tilhørende statsapparat er udviklet med rigelige olieindtægter som et grundvilkår.

Målet med afhandlingen er at analysere social og økonomisk udvikling i de arabiske golfstater det seneste halve århundrede. Mere specifikt analyserer jeg udvalgte aspekter af den udviklingssti (development trajectory), de arabiske golfstater har fulgt, følger eller planlægger at følge. Med udviklingsstien forstår jeg "... the patterns of economic change and structural transformation manifested in a society" (Cammett et al. 2015, 9).

På baggrund af disse analyser søger jeg med afhandlingen at bidrage både teoretisk og empirisk til at fremme videnskaben inden for det akademiske fagområde, der benævnes 'Social science-based Gulf Studies' eller på dansk 'samfundsvidenskabelige golfstudier.'

Afhandling er tværvidenskabelig og placerer sig i grænselandet mellem to akademiske hovedområder: humaniora og samfundsvidenskab. Mens humaniora, og i særdeleshed fagdisciplinen historie, har en lang tradition bag sig både inden for mellemøststudier og golfstudier, er samfundsvidenskabelig forskning, der beskæftiger sig med nutidige politiske, økonomiske og sociale problemstillinger i Golflandene, fortsat meget ung og uudviklet både teoretisk og empirisk. Det er der en række grunde til. Vigtigst blandt dem er en signifikant mangel på data og som følge heraf også viden om de samfund, der studeres. Det er håbet, at denne afhandling vil medvirke til at bringe samfundsvidenskabelige golfstudier et lille skridt videre, da afhandlingen bygger på et betydeligt feltarbejde foretaget over en længere årrække, at der i afhandlingen introduceres nye typer datakilder, samt at der bringes en teori i anvendelsen, der er ny inden for forskningsfeltet.

Afhandlingen er inspireret af og udtænkt inden for rammerne af to forskningsområder. På den ene side mellemøststudier/golfstudier og på den anden udviklingsøkonomi. Herudover baserer denne afhandling sig på en specifik epistemologisk tilgang, nemlig områdestudie-tilgangen. Afhandlingens analyser befinder sig således i krydsfeltet, som angivet i Figur 1.

Figure 1. Afhandlingens teoretiske og faglige ramme

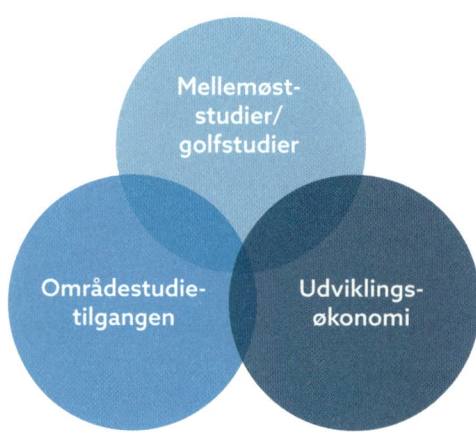

Mellemøststudier/golfstudier repræsenterer den overordnede forskningstradition, dens paradigmer, dens teoretiske tilgange og dens institutionalisering. Områdestudie-tilgangen repræsenterer en specifik epistemologisk tilgang, som er indlejret i golfstudier. Udviklingsøkonomi er en samfundsvidenskabelig disciplin, som sætter fokus på samfundsmæssig udvikling og planlægning. Tilgangen definerer de specifikke emner i hver af de analyser, jeg foretager af de respektive publikationer, og leverer de teorier og del-teorier, der anvendes.

Afhandlingen består af fire hovedafsnit. Det første redegør for de tre ovenfornævnte elementer i afhandlingens teoretiske og faglige ramme. Det andet hovedafsnit resumerer indholdet af de inkluderede publikationer og forskningsresultaterne fra hver af publikationerne. Det tredje hovedafsnit er det forskningsmæssigt tungeste og udgøres af de ni inkluderede publikationer. Den fjerde og sidste del er den nærværende tekst, der er et kort resumé af afhandlingen affattet på dansk. Det omhandler de tre elementer i afhandlingens teoretiske og faglige ramme samt et resumé af afhandlingens væsentligste bidrag til forskningen.

Mellemøststudier/golfstudier

Studier af Golflandene, både i deres helhed og den samfundsvidenskabelige del af disse, fremstår i dag som et meget ungt og umodent forskningsområde. Med stiftelsen af 'Association for Gulf and Arabian Peninsula Studies' (AGAPS) i 2011 blev studierne af de arabiske golflande etableret som et særskilt forskningsområde under det bredere forskningsfelt: mellemøststudier.

Mens arkæologiske, historiske og etnografiske studier af Golflandene og deres befolkning er blevet udført i det 19. og 20. århundrede, er det først inden for de seneste årtier, at samfundsvidenskabelig forskning, som er rettet mod landenes økonomiske, sociale og politiske spørgsmål, er vokset i størrelse, både hvad angår mængden af forskere, der beskæftiger sig med regionen, og ikke mindst i antallet af publikationer.

Mens der er mange lighedstræk mellem forskning, der udføres i forskningsfeltet mellemøststudier og i studierne af Golflandene, vil jeg afgrænse denne afhandling til de samfundsvidenskabeligt orienterede golfstudier. Det vil jeg gøre gennem en analyse af de træk, der adskiller de to fagområder. I afhandlingen argumenteres der for, at der er tre træk, der på afgørende vis adskiller de to fagområder: 1) en signifikant mangel på data, 2) én dominerende teori og 3) en række særlige forskningsemner.

Grundlæggende data som for eksempel befolkningsstørrelse, arbejdsstyrkens etniske sammensætning, statsbudgetter, økonomiske nøgletal, indkomstdata med videre er enten ikke tilgængelige eller kun gjort tilgængelige for offentligheden i 'high-light'-versioner. Endnu mere mangelfulde og usystematisk indsamlet er data på mindre aggregerede niveauer for eksempel vedrørende indkomstfordeling, uddannelses- eller sundhedssystemer, virksomhedsdata, ejerskab af jord eller ejendomme, overførsel af sociale ydelser med videre.

Mens alle forskere, der studerer økonomier under udvikling, står over for problemer med at skaffe pålidelige data, argumenterer jeg i denne afhandling for, at problemet er særligt udtalt for forskere, der arbejder med Golflandene. Det er der fire grunde til: 1) Samfundenes konstituering, hvor autokratiske og neo-patrimoniale styreformer indskrænker eller direkte modvirker offentlig debat, fremvækst af interessegrupper og i det hele taget gennemsigtighed i beslutningsprocesser, 2) begrænset statslig kapacitet i forhold til at indsamle data som følge af, at der stort set ikke er etableret beskatningssystemer, 3) en begrænset inddragelse af internationale organisationer i økonomien for eksempel gennem medlemskab af sådanne organisationer, långivning og indgåede traktater. Alle faktorer, der mindsker kravet til åbenhed om data og udarbejdelse af statistisk materiale, 4) og endelig den fortsatte tilstedeværelse af en mundtlig kultur, hvilket indebærer, at der ikke er tradition for at indsamle data, opbygge arkiver eller indsamle andre vidnesbyrd på skrift. En konsekvens heraf er, at de væsentligste kilder til samfundsudviklingen og statsdannelsesprocesserne i det 19. og 20. århundrede er udarbejdet af embedsmænd i det britiske kolonistyre.

Denne mangel på basale statistiske oplysninger, og den politiske sensitivitet, som både data og forskning er omgivet af, er selvsagt en betydelig hindring for forskningen. Uden data kan hverken landenes myndigheder eller forskerne opnå systematisk viden. En konsekvens heraf er, at samfundsvidenskabelige studier med et nutidigt fokus, som i denne afhandling, oftest er baseret på kvalitative dataindsamlingsteknikker i form af interviews.

Manglen på data har hæmmet videnopbygningen og dermed forskningsfeltets mulighed for at opstille teorier. Som sådan fremstår det videnskabelige felt af samfundsvidenskabeligt orienterede studier af Golflandene både som ungt og umodent.

På det teoretiske plan adskiller studierne af Golflandene sig fra mellemøststudier ved dominansen af én teori: rentierstatsteorien (Rentier State Theory). Denne har de sidste 30 år udgjort den teoretiske linse, gennem hvilken samfundsvidenskabelige forskere forstår økonomiske og politiske dynamikker i Golflandene, herunder forholdet mellem borger og samfund. Rentierstatsteorien fremstår ikke som én samlet teori, men som en række konsekvenser, primært af negativ art, forbundet med en hurtig og massiv tilstrømning af 'utjente' penge fra olie- og gasproduktionen. Konsekvenserne omfatter 'Dutch disease,' 'crowding out' processer og fremvæksten af en ikke-produktionsorienteret tankegang, den såkaldte 'rentier mentalitet.'

Teorien forklarer fremvæksten af 'distributive stater,' der er karakteriseret ved stater, hvor indkomsten fra olie eller gas er dominerende i økonomien, og hvor statens væsentligste rolle består i at fordele disse indtægter i samfundene. Teorien har endvidere været anvendt til at forklare regimestabilitet i Golflandene. Teorien peger på, at fraværet af folkelig repræsentation i statslige beslutningsprocesser skyldes, at der ikke opkræves skat fra befolkningen. 'No taxation, no representation,' som teorien argumenterer. Teorien er under betydelig kritik. Dels for at være statisk og dels for at være for unuanceret i sine analyser af de politiske processer. I denne afhandling bruger jeg dele af teorien i mine analyser, og jeg bidrager desuden til kritikken af teorien ved blandt andet at påvise, hvordan beslutningstagere i regionen ikke blot passivt uddelte olierigdomme til befolkningen, som forudsat i teorien, men faktisk gennem planlægning og implementering af projekter har gjort aktive forsøg på at skabe en diversificeret og bæredygtig økonomi.

Slutteligt argumenteres der i afhandlingen for, at samfundsvidenskabeligt orienterede golfstudier adskiller sig fra mellemøststudier i valget af de problemstillinger, der forskes i. Jeg argumenterer i afhandlingen for, at der er tre overordnede emner, der karakteriserer golfstudier: 1) studier, der har deres udgangspunkt i de forskellige 'oliekriser', og som omhandler olie- og gassektoren i Golflandene, industrien som helhed og dets hovedaktører, 2) studier af internationale forhold og sikkerhedsspørgsmål relateret til regionens rolle som global leverandør af olie, krigene i regionen (Iran-Irak-krigen i 1980-1988, Iraks besættelse af Kuwait i 1990, den amerikansk ledede koalition for at befri Kuwait i 1991 og senere fjernelsen af Saddam Hussein i 2003) samt den tiltagende konkurrence mellem Iran og Saudi Arabien om, hvilket land der skal være leder i regionen, 3) og slutteligt studier, der relaterer sig til den eksplosive vækst, regionen har gennemgået i perioden 1999-2014 på det økonomiske, sociale og kulturelle plan. Emnemæssigt indplacerer min afhandling sig i den tredje kategori.

Afgrænsningen af forskningsfeltet 'samfundsvidenskabeligt orienterede golfstudier' tjener to formål i afhandlingen. Først definerer den det forskningsområde, som jeg i afhandlingen yder et forskningsmæssigt bidrag til. Dernæst bidrager den til at påpege de begrænsninger, som forskere inden for feltet møder i deres forskning (manglen på data, systematisk viden om samfundene og underteoretiseringen). De publikationer, afhandlingen består af, er skrevet over de sidste 15 år og den reflekterer således disses begrænsning og deres udvikling over tid. De forskningsspørgsmål, der adresseres, og de resultater, der er opnået i publikationerne, er desuden et udtryk for en dialog mellem feltets empiriske og teoretiske udvikling.

Områdestudie-tilgangen

Epistemologisk baserer min afhandling sig på områdestudie-tilgangen. Det indebærer, at den er tværfaglig, har et partikularistisk tilsnit, da den tillægger empirisk og kontekstuel viden betydning som fundament for opbygningen af robuste teorier, og slutteligt fokuserer på nutidigt og politisk relevant indhold. Områdestudie-tilgangen indeholder således et nomotetisk mål, dog mindre udpræget end i de rene discipliner som for eksempel politologi og økonomi.

Denne epistemologiske tilgang ser jeg som nødvendig grundet forskningsfeltets ringe udviklingsgrad. For det første betyder manglen på data, at den skarpe opdeling mellem fagdisciplinerne i for eksempel økonomi, politik, kultur og samfund, som er mulig i mere udviklede samfund, ikke er mulig for landene i denne region. For det andet udgør den samfundsmæssige virkelighed i Golfstaterne en uigennemskuelig blanding af formelle styreformer (repræsenteret af sheiker, de herskende familier og eliterne) overlejret af familie- og stammestrukturer samt tillige af stærke kulturelle normer bundet op på religion. Jeg argumenterer i afhandlingen for, at denne samfundsmæssige virkelighed gør det umuligt at foretage en meningsfuld skelnen mellem politik, økonomi og kultur, hvorfor en tværfaglig og partikularistisk tilgang nødvendigvis må bringes i anvendelse, når man studerer disse samfund.

Udviklingsøkonomi

Det tredje element i afhandlingens teoretiske og faglige ramme er disciplinen udviklingsøkonomi. Denne disciplin har præget afhandlingen på forskellig vis.

For det første har den udviklingsøkonomiske tilgang betydet, at jeg i afhandlingen fokuserer på udvikling og forandring. For eksempel er jeg ikke optaget af økonomisk diversificering, statsreformer eller opbygning af human kapital i sig selv. I stedet er jeg optaget af, hvordan disse faktorer hver især og samlet har kunnet bidrage til langsigtet vækst og til udvikling i Golflandene. Dette perspektiv indebærer, at virkninger eller resultater af analyserne skal vurderes i forhold til den potentielle indvirkning på langsigtet vækst og udvikling.

For det andet indebærer det udviklingsøkonomiske fokus, at analyseenheden er samfundet som helhed, og ikke den enkelte borger, virksomheden eller sektor.

For det tredje er der en tidsdimension forbundet med samfundsmæssig udvikling, da virkninger af politiske tiltag måske først viser sig på mellemlang eller lang sigt. På braudelsk vis betyder et udviklingsorienteret fokus en nedprioritering af betydningen af daglige politiske hændelser til fordel for de mere langsigtede perspektiver på for eksempel opbygningen af et lands konkurrenceevne, eller hvordan den næste generation af borgere bliver forberedt på at indgå i fremtidens videnssamfund. Denne tilgang er understøttet af det institutionelle fokus i afhandlingen.

For det fjerde har fagdisciplinen udviklingsøkonomi givet min afhandling fokus på økonomisk udvikling og især de forskellige (del)-teorier, som er taget i anvendelse i de studier, der er inkluderet i afhandlingen. Det være sig Hirschmans ([1958] 1969) dynamik vedrørende 'fremad- og bagudrettede linkages' i forbindelse med industriel vækst, Kuznets' (1967, 1973) arbejder omkring strukturelle transformationer, Porters (1998) bidrag om industrielle klynger, Rosenstein-Rodans (1943) 'Big push' omhandlende koordination af investeringer, Schumpeters (1961) iværksættere og den deraf følgende 'ceative destruction' og mere bredt 'udviklingsstatsteori', som idémæssigt følger i fodsporene på forskere som Polany ([1944] 2001), Gerschenkron ([1962] 1966) og Evans (1989, 1995).

Med andre ord definerer udviklingsøkonomi som disciplin i vid udstrækning de specifikke emner, som adresseres i hver af publikationerne inkluderet i afhandlingen. Endvidere fastlægger disciplinen det eksplicitte fokus på samfundsmæssig udvikling, den underliggende (neo)klassiske opfattelse af økonomisk adfærd og ikke mindst de teorier, der bringes i anvendelse. Fagdisciplinen udviklingsøkonomi lider dog af flere svagheder. Ifølge Martinussen (2005, 353) har udviklingsøkonomi ikke været i stand til at opstille overordnede teorier eller modeller for vækst og udvikling med gyldighed for alle tredjeverdenslande. Således fremstår fagdisciplinens teoretiske bidrag hovedsageligt som mellemniveau-teorier.

Resumé af opnåede forskningsresultater

I afhandlingens anden hoveddel opsummerer jeg de ni publikationer, som afhandlingen omfatter. Her redegør jeg for deres respektive bidrag til forskningen inden for de samfundsvidenskabeligt orienterede golfstudier. Samlet set mener jeg med denne afhandling at have bidraget til videreudviklingen af forskningsområdet på følgende punkter:

For det første ved at introducere 'udviklingsstatsteorien' som et alternativt teoretisk perspektiv til den hegemoniske 'rentierstatsteori' i studiet af Golflandene. Udviklingsstatsteorien tillægger staten en afgørende betydning som drivkraft i samfundsudviklingen (statisme) og fokuserer på effektiv 'statecraft' og på, hvad Evans (1995, 6) kalder statens 'transformative rolle'; det vil sige statens kapacitet til at facilitere iværksætteri og dermed skabelsen af nye produkter og produktion. Teorien tillægger således staten en dynamisk og proaktiv rolle og postulerer, at vækst og velstand ikke længere bør ses som en funktion af naturen og markederne, men som noget, der kan skabes gennem statslige indgreb.

Udviklingsstatsteorien er udviklet til at analysere væksten i de asiatiske 'tiger-økonomier' i anden del af det 20. århundrede. Den har desuden vist sig yderst anvendelig både som et analytisk og forklarende redskab i mine studier i denne afhandling. Golflandenes centraliserede beslutningsstruktur, sene start på deres udviklingsproces, målsætning om at indhente Vesten og ikke mindst de midler, Golflandene råder over til at udvikle 'created comparative advantages' rammer centralt i dette teoretiske perspektiv.

I min afhandling anvender jeg udviklingsstatsteorien til analysen af statens forankring i samfundet (embeddedness), hvilket konkret udmønter sig i en analyse af de formelle og i særdeleshed de uformelle bånd, der sammenbinder væsentlige aktører som handelsstanden og de ledende eliter i de arabiske golflande. Endvidere er udviklingsstatsteorien lagt til grund for de analyser, der fokuserer på staternes kapacitet og effektiviteten af deres bureaukratier.

Udviklingsstatsteorien kan potentielt føre til alternative forklaringer på den observerede vækst, som rentierstatsteorien giver. Dog betyder manglen på data, og indsigt i hvordan Golflandenes statsbureaukratier løser deres opgaver, at anvendelsen af udviklingsstatsteorien endnu ikke har nået sit fulde potentiale.

Afhandlingen yder desuden et teoretisk bidrag til forskningen gennem en eksplicit kritik af rentierstatsteorien. I klassisk rentierstatsteori indtager beslutningstagere i rentierstaterne rollen som passive distributører af (ubegrænsede) olieformuer. Med mine empiriske studier har jeg påvist, at dette ikke er tilfældet. Derimod dokumenterer afhandlingen, hvordan staterne og beslutningstagerne har forsøgt - nogle endog meget ivrigt - at placere deres lande på en udviklingssti med diversificerede økonomier ved at reformere økonomierne i retning af en produktionsorienteret økonomisk orden og for dermed at give deres økonomier et mere solidt fodfæste.

Endvidere argumenter jeg i afhandlingen for, at fremvæksten af samfundsplanlægning i Golfstaterne over det seneste 10 år (Oman og Saudi Arabien dog med en tidligere start) er et klart vidnesbyrd om, at staten ikke spiller en passiv rolle, men må ses som spillende en aktiv rolle i udviklingen. Planlægning og implementering af planer, af fysisk, økonomisk eller social art, er et udtryk for et ønske om at gennemføre ændringer, der forhåbentligt betyder forbedringer for samfundet og dets borgere. Med andre ord bygger staternes planlægning på en formodning om ønskværdig handling og statslig handlekraft. Hermed negerer afhandlingens analyser af planlægning og implementering af planer rentierstatsteoriens forudsætning vedrørende den passive stat.

Slutteligt udgør det eksplicitte institutionelle fokus, og i særdeleshed den historiske institutionalisme, i afhandlingen et bidrag til forskningsfeltet. Institutionelle analyser har kun i meget beskedent omfang været appliceret som teoretisk og analytisk værktøj af andre forskere inden for golfstudier. I afhandlingen anskuer jeg institutioner som permanente træk i den historisk udvikling, hvorved jeg har åbent op for analyser af det dynamiske samspil mellem historiske perioder karakteriseret af 'sti-afhængighed' og 'kritiske tidspunkter.'

Den økonomiske virkelighed i Golflandene har været præget af markante ændringer over det seneste århundrede såsom briternes kolonisering og siden afkolonisering, perleindustriens afvikling, fremvæksten af olieindustrien og de radikale samfundsændringer, som olieindtægterne gjorde muligt. Anvendelsen af et institutionelt fokus har bidraget til en historisk identifikation af de lange udviklingsstier og dermed bidraget til en dybere forståelse af mulighederne og hindringerne for forandringer både på samfundsmæssigt og individuelt plan.

På det empiriske plan bidrager mit arbejde i afhandlingen til at definere, dokumentere og analysere 'Dubai-modellen for økonomisk udvikling.' Ved sin publicering i 2009 gav denne model et hidtil ikke eksisterende referencepunkt for drøftelser og analyser af udviklingsstien – ikke kun i Dubai, men mere generelt i Golfstaterne.

Desuden har jeg med denne afhandling introduceret analyser af statslig planlægning i Golflandene. Målet hermed har været at opnå en systematisk forståelse for nutidige og fremtidige samfundsmæssige mål og prioriteringer. Parallelt med studierne af planlægning i Golflandene har afhandlingen introduceret udviklingsplaner som brugbare og legitime tekstbaserede kilder.

Endelig har min forskning placeret Golflandene i udviklingssekvensen som 'late-late-late developere' og påvist, hvilke mulighederne og begrænsninger denne sene start på udviklingsprocessen har haft for udviklingsvalgene og dermed de udviklingsstier, som landene har kunnet følge.

I erkendelsen af, at udvikling er en multikausal proces, har jeg opbygget min afhandling omkring en række emner og teorier, der er centrale for, hvad Stern (1989, 669) betegner som 'grand issues' inden for disciplinen udviklingsøkonomi: statsstrukturer, institutioner, udviklingsparadigmer og -planlægning og indkomstgenererende aktiviteter for eksempel naturressourcer, industrialisering og tjenesteydelser. Hertil kommer demografisk vækst og opbygning af human kapital, arbejdsmarkedsspørgsmål, migration og endelig international handel, globalisering, betalingsbalanceproblemer og investeringer.

Hver af de vedlagte studier er således at betragte som byggesten i en større struktur, der udgør puljen af kvalificeret teoretisk og empirisk viden relateret til den udviklingssti, de moderne arabiske golfstater har fulgt og ønsker at følge.

Jeg erkender, at ovenstående redegørelse for de videnskabelige bidrag, jeg mener at have opnået i denne afhandling, kan læses som et udtryk for manglende akademisk beskedenhed. Indenfor modne forskningsområder vil det sjældent forekomme, at en forsker kan hævde at være den første til at introducere en teori eller et kildemateriale. Inden for golfstudier har situationen dog været anderledes. Først og fremmest fordi golfstudier er et både ungt og umodent forskningsområde, hvilke muliggør mange 'firsts' eller 'news' til de forskere, der er med i den tidlige opbygning af området.

For det andet fordi min akademiske baggrund som geograf og udviklingsøkonom repræsenterer et særegent forskningsfokus inden for golfstudierne. Forskningsfeltet er domineret af forskere med baggrund i fagdisciplinen historie og i mindre grad antropologi og statskundskab, hvorfor afhandlingens analyser, der relaterer sig til planlægning og udviklingsøkonomi, i vid udstrækning er faldet uden for andre forskeres interesseområder. Netop derfor har der været et stort uopdyrket forskningsområde for den type studier, som min faglige specialisering muliggør.

5 Summary in Danish/Dansk resumé

På det metodiske plan repræsenterer afhandling en normalisering af analyserne af Golfstaterne, idet jeg ikke behandler udviklingen i de arabiske golfstater som eksotisk eller på anden vis som stående uden for den normale humanistiske eller samfundsvidenskabelige forskning. Metoden bygger på en universalistisk tilgang, hvor generelle teorier og metodologiske værktøjer er anvendt, hvilket har gjort det muligt at lave komparative analyser blandt de seks golflande og mellem golflandene og andre lande under udvikling. På sigt ser jeg store perspektiver i komparative analyser af for eksempel udvikling inden for 'capital rich'-stater eller af variation inden for de mål og værktøjer, som benyttes blandt forskellige udviklingsstater. Endeligt kan komparative analyser anvendes i forhold til udviklingsstater, der kan hidrøre fra traditionelle styreformer.

Men selv fra et universalistisk perspektiv har denne gruppe af lande egenskaber, der gør dem forskellige fra andre lande under udvikling, nemlig deres sene start på udviklingsprocessen, den betydelige mængde kapital, de har til deres rådighed for at understøtte deres udviklingsproces, og endelig, med undtagelse af Saudi-Arabien, en meget lille befolkning i hvert land. Disse faktorer har skabt en kontekst for deres udvikling, som er væsensforskellig fra de fleste andre udviklingslande.

Cammett et al. (2015, 23ff) argumenterer for, at der eksisterer en sammenhæng mellem ressourcerigelighed og politisk udvikling i de mellemøstlige stater. Jeg opstiller den hypotese, at der eksisterer en sammenhæng mellem ressourcerigelighed og økonomisk udvikling i Golflandene.

Mens flere ressourcerige lande for eksempel Irak, Iran, Libyen, Syrien, og uden for regionen især Nigeria og Venezuela, har haft betydelige problemer med at omsætte høje olieindtægter til udvikling, ser det ikke ud til at være tilfældet i de arabiske golfstater. På det overordnede niveau finder jeg i denne afhandling grund til at antage, at der eksisterer en sammenhæng mellem ressourcerigelighed og økonomisk udvikling i de arabiske golfstater. Det skyldes ikke alene indkomsternes størrelse, men også de refordelingsmekanismer, der er indlejret den traditionelle familie-, stamme- og rentierbaserede organisering af samfundene.

Der er ikke mangel på eksempler på, hvordan olierigdommen er blevet formøblet, hvordan olieindkomsten fortsat bidrager til at opretholde en ekstremt ulige indkomstfordeling, og hvordan indtægterne har været medvirkende til at forhindre eller udsætte nødvendige økonomiske reformer. Men på den anden side har de herskende eliter i Golflandene bevidst kanaliseret massive beløb til forbedring af samfundets levestandard som helhed og til en bredere udviklingsproces, som i de seneste 50 år har været blandt de hurtigste i verden. Statistikker relateret til parametrene indeholdt i HDI-indekset, det vil sige forventet levealder ved fødsel, spædbarns dødelighed og antal års skolegang, vidner alle om massive udviklingsfremskridt siden begyndelsen af 1970'erne.

Afhandlingen anerkender og bifalde denne positive udvikling. Dog har de undersøgelser og analyser, der er udført i afhandlingen, hovedsageligt fokuseret på de problematiske følgevirkninger af den økonomiske anomali, der er skabt af den pludselige og massive tilstrømning af indtægter fra olien gennem de sidste 50 år. Mens landene har gjort sig betydelige anstrengelser for at skabe en diversificeret økonomi, der har kunnet skabe beskæftigelse, også til den lokale befolkning og gøre økonomierne mindre sårbare, er Golflandenes afhængighed af olien som indtægtskilde ikke faldet. Tværtimod er den blevet ved med at stige over årene. Således er hovedproblemstillingen fortsat hvordan, og ikke mindst hvornår, Golflandene foretager en samfundsmæssig kursændring, der vil bringe dem på en udviklingssti, der er økonomisk og socialt bæredygtig.

Referencer

Cammett, Melani, Ishac Diwan, Alan Richards, and John Waterbury. 2015. *A Political Economy of The Middle East*. Boulder, Colorado: Westview Press.

Evans, Peter B. 1989. "Predatory, Developmental and Other Apparatuses: A comparative Political Economy Perspective on the Third World State." *Sociological Forum* 4 (4): 561-87.

———. 1995. *Embedded Autonomy: States and Industrial Transformation*. New Jersey: Princeton University Press.

Gerschenkron, Alexander. [1962] 1966. *Economic Backwardness in Historical Perspective. A Book of Essays*. Cambridge, Massachusetts: The Belknap Press of Harvard University Press.

Kuznets, Simon. 1967. *Modern Economic Growth: Rate Structure, and Spread*. New Haven and London: Yale University Press.

———. 1973. "Modern Economic Growth: Findings and Reflections." *The American Economic Review* 63 (3): 247-58.

Martinussen, John Degnbol. 2005. *Society, State & Market: A Guide to Competing Theories of Development*. London: Zed Books.

Polany, Karl. [1944] 2001. *The Great Transformation: The Political and Economic Origins of Our Time*. Boston: Beacon Press.

Porter, Michael E. 1998. "Clusters and the New Economics of Competition." *Harvard Business Review* (November-December 1998): 77–90.

Rosenstein-Rodan, Paul N. 1943. "Problems of Industrialisation of Eastern and South-Eastern Europe." *The Economic Journal* 53 (210/211): 202-11.

Schumpeter, Joseph A. 1961. *The Theory of Economic Development: An Inquiry into Profits, Capital, Credit, Interest, and the Business Cycle.* New York: Oxford University Press.

Stern, Nicholas. 1989. "The Economics of Development: A Survey." *The Economic Journal* 99 (397): 597-685.